It All Ends Up in a Parfait Glass

A TRIBUTE TO MY MOTHER'S WISDOM

MARJIE ZACKS

It All Ends Up in A Parfait Glass
Copyright © 2022 Marjie Zacks

No part of this publication may be reproduced or transmitted in any form or by any means, electronic or mechanical, including photocopying, recording or by any information storage and retrieval system, now known or to be invented, without permission in writing from the publisher.

Published by Marjie Zacks
Contact: mszacks53@gmail.com

ISBN: 978-1-7782553-0-4 (softcover)
ISBN: 978-1-7782553-1-1 (eBook)

Edited by Marial Shea
Cover and text design by Tania Craan
eBook produced by Jan Westendorp/www.katodesignandphoto.com

CONTENTS
· · · · · · · · · · ·

Introduction 7

1. What did you accomplish today? 9

2. What would the neighbours say? 12

3. Look it up! 15

4. Next to me, I love you best 17

5. Everything was butter-side down 19

6. Oh, you know, a little of this and a little of that! 21

7. Hanging out our teeth together 23

8. You can't make a silk purse out of a sow's ear 25

9. A bad beginning is a good ending 28

10. Fleeing the Cossacks . . . abandoning everything 31

11. On a bicycle built for two 35

12. Smile and the world smiles with you. Cry and you cry alone 37

13. The white lie 39

14. You be the bigger person 42

15. Comfortable in one's own skin 44

16. It all ends up in a parfait glass 47

17. **Sweet sixteen** 49

18. **Happy birthday, Harvey!** 52

19. **Good grammar, good grief!** 55

20. **Laughter through tears, or tears of laughter** 57

21. **Sweet legacy** 61

22. **Keeping house** 64

23. **Help is a four-letter word. Why?** 69

24. **Your eyes were bigger than your stomach** 72

25. **Never close a door so tight you can't get your foot in it again** 75

26. **One day you will** 78

27. **Small-town kid meets big city** 81

28. **You can choose your friends but you can't choose your family** 84

29. **Plan B** 86

30. **Putting your best foot forward ... may have something to do with your footwear** 89

31. **Nothing is ever black or white ... unless it is** 93

32. **Don't shoot yourself in the foot!** 96

33. **Looking like you just stepped out of a bandbox** 99

34. **'Twas the week before Chanukah (during a pandemic)** 103

35. **Monday comes the revolution!** 106

36. **"Don't worry, I'm fine, dear"** 109

37. **Rugelach reminiscences** 114

38. **High time for high tea** 116

39. **No good deed goes unpunished!** 119

40. **Cross that bridge when you come to it ... or,
Get out of the buggy, Becky; you're not there yet** 122

41. **Christmas ... a time of giving even if it's not our holiday** 125

42. **Cabbage rolls hold many secrets** 128

43. **Twenty-twenty hindsight** 132

44. **Once again it is Passover** 137

45. **The truth about memory** 141

Afterword 144

Acknowledgements 146

Introduction

Although my mom passed away over twelve years ago, I recently found myself revisiting a number of her expressions remembered from my childhood. The more I mulled over these sayings, the more I marveled at their wisdom. To honour my mother's memory, I wanted to share her funniest expressions — what we thought of them back then as youngsters, what we know them to mean now as adults and what she, herself, would say if she were still alive today. I also wanted to share these memories with my sister, who has very few recollections of her own childhood. These stories about growing up in the 1950s and '60s have thus morphed into a book. I'm certain there were many other families like ours, but every family thinks theirs was surely original.

Life is so different today, but no matter how much the world has changed, the ongoing relevance of those utterances from so long ago still impresses me. They reflect themes common to anyone who has grown up, and contain life lessons that continue to resonate to this day. Those lessons impart the importance of making the best of a bad situation, following a moral code, respecting the elderly and authority, and self-love. They also emphasize achievement, independence, perseverance, female empowerment, community and the very human need to belong.

It may now be a good sixty years later but my mother's priceless phrases still make me stop and think, sometimes with humour, sometimes in awe and always with respect for the wisdom they contain. I hope they will do so for you too.

1

What did you accomplish today?

My family came from a long line of accomplishers. My grandfather was somewhat of a religious leader in his community, back in the Old Country. He was also a successful businessman. When my grandmother sent my father, aged twelve, on a train from Poland to Liverpool, and from there on a steamer ship to Saint John, New Brunswick, Canada, it was with the understanding that he would make something of himself in the New World. My mother, whose parents arrived in Boston from Latvia, came from very humble circumstances. Her father was a carpenter and her mother a caterer who would sometimes extend credit to her clients well beyond what she could afford. In far corners of the U.S.A. there are delicatessens still serving her famous chopped-liver recipe. But I digress...

My father completed high school in three years, my mother in two. My father went off to medical school and my mother, not knowing initially that she had won a scholarship, changed her plan to enter secretarial school at the last minute in order to attend law school instead, something for which you did not need an undergraduate degree in the thirties. My mom started off teaching the bar review course for law students, then moved to Washington, D.C., as the assistant rent review attorney for New England. You get the point. These two worked very hard for every success and were not the type of people who suffered fools easily.

From a young age, and through their own first-hand experience, my parents believed that education was the only way to succeed in life, and they constantly pushed us to be better than our best. No average results would do. My sister, the compliant first-born, was good at school. Not so much her younger sibling — *moi*. According to my parents, I was very bright, if only I would apply myself. Then there were the requisite extra-curricular activities. I took ballet, tap and baton, but I was a *klutz* and had no real aspirations to become a dancer in a tutu. Piano lessons terrified me so much that my hands shook on the keys during weekly lessons. As for swimming lessons, I was so scared of going under that my folks had to pay the swim teacher to drag me around the pool with the promise to never let me go. He lied and I almost drowned. Suffice to say I was just an average kid in a not so average family. But, yikes, I delighted in mischief and weekends. Yet summer camp was a nightmare for me, and I was homesick from the get-go.

It wasn't until many years later that I learned how ingrained in my parents was this desire for accomplishment. I was then in Israel, in my thirties, and had recently returned to my cousin's home after a day of sightseeing. She did not say, "How was it? How are you? How was your day?" No, the first words out of her mouth were, "So, what did you accomplish today?" She too had clearly been raised in a family obsessed with the notion of accomplishment. Of course she had. Her mom and my dad had the same driven parents. We were first cousins, after all. I guess it's genetic. The pair of us talked about that for hours.

Daydreaming was not permitted in my parents' home. Instead, it was, "Why don't you read a book?"

A chance to be idle during the summer? No way. "Get a job," my dad urged when I was seventeen and thought a summer off would be nice

When time came for university, I didn't want to go. What was the point? I had no ambition to be or do anything. I was too young. But my dad insisted. He said I would figure it out as I went along. And I did. The downside of it all? To this day I find it very hard to just sit and do nothing. A therapist once told me I was a human *being*, not a human *doing*. And I try to remember that as I tally up my activities at a day's end. I still feel a bit disappointed in myself if the day was not full of productivity and accomplishment, even if the day in question included painting, reading, working out or cooking. Until I retired I was working, often late into the night, at a more than full-time career in public relations.

While that constant need to feel I have accomplished something is a lasting legacy from my parents, I realize that I can't necessarily be as driven as they were, even though I never would want to disappoint them. I try very hard not to feel guilty when I hear their voices in my ear, long after they have gone. I wonder what they are cooking up there in the Great Beyond. They are probably saying to their friends, "Don't just sit there. Accomplish something!"

2

What would the neighbours say?

If we were out playing in the street — yes, in those days we did, and quite safely too except maybe for an errant baseball bat hitting us by accident — we were to *keep our voices down.* Whether our mother felt our behaviour inappropriate for polite society or whether hearing kids laughing and playing in the street offended her academic sensibilities, we were always told, *"Your voices are the only ones I can hear out there, yelling and shrieking."* Truth was, our mother, like most mothers, was probably more attuned to her own offspring's voices than to anyone else's kids. No matter who else was out yelling and *"carrying on"* on our street, we were the ones who were always told to behave.

Our neighbours across the street, a boy my age and a girl my sister's age, were once invited to come over for dinner when their parents were out of town. We laughed and giggled our way throughout dinner itself, but when it came to dessert, the serious business of eating brownies, I completely lost it. Brownies were coming out of my nose and mouth as I collapsed in a fit of hysterics. I immediately got *the look* from my dad, the one where he raised his eyes over the glasses resting on his nose, but otherwise didn't move his head. That glance was enough to kill: I was banished from the table.

No wonder, many years later, my childhood friends confided in me that they were terrified of coming to dinner at our home. They didn't know which fork to use, so were fearful of committing a grave culinary misdemeanor. Who knew? My friends divulged this information to me long after my parents were gone.

Reflecting on my own experiences as a mom, some of my happiest times at my own table in my own kitchen were with my daughter, my cousin and her son, who was my daughter's age. One of the youngsters would start, and then the other would burst into fits of laughter, much to the disapproval of his mom. After my upbringing, kids laughing at the table over complete nonsense was a rare gift and, being the well-brought-up lady that I was not, I just cracked up right along with the kids, feeling very much like a misbehaving child myself. My cousin was mortified, of course, but I just laughed along and invited them both time and again for repeat performances.

I think that absolutely no emphasis is put on table manners today. You just have to go into a restaurant with young children sitting nearby and see that, not only do the parents let the kids entertain themselves with screens rather than conversation, but they also don't insist that the kids lower their voices. In those instances, I automatically channel my mother — Shhhhh. Yours are the only voices I can hear. Not so loud. Tone it down. More to the point, I can barely hear my own self think, never mind carry on a conversation.

The times sure have changed. Nothing makes me happier than passing a schoolyard during recess, full of kids all running, playing and, yes, shrieking. It reminds me of how important it is for us to hang on to the fun part of our childhoods. But, as I learned from my own folks, there is a time and a place. I don't worry so much about my own behaviour any more, or what the neighbours think, but it sure is hard to overcome your upbringing. Not all of those long-ago lessons should be thrown out with the bathwater.

LEFT TO RIGHT: *Me with our friends Gail Abramsky and David Abramsky, and my sister, Ellie, in 1959.*

3

Look it up!

Whether we were appearing busy or, more often, eavesdropping on conversations we were not meant to overhear, "Look it up" was the response if we asked what a word meant, and no definition was ever forthcoming. I think our mother firmly believed in not doing anything for us that we could do for ourselves. Or perhaps she was just too busy. The response expected from us was to go to the dictionary and look the mystery word up. Not knowing how to spell it made looking it up difficult — or in my case, not wanting to read anything in the first place meant that my parents' suggestion fell on deaf ears. I walked away still ignorant or, in my mind substituting whatever I thought the meaning should be.

I would always rather be playing outside in the street: tag, hide-and-seek, baseball, football. Not so my older sister, the bookworm. She probably dutifully looked up everything and she spent her time behind the closed door of her bedroom for a good chunk of my childhood. Being three years my senior put her and her friends beyond reach of us socializing together. Tolerating me was an option only when she had no one else around. One thing we both agreed on was that our parents were driven people, not only in terms of their own lives, but in what they wanted for us as well. (See chapter 1, "What did you accomplish today?")

Telling us to look up the words we did not understand was probably their well-meant attempt at making us more independent and trying to instil in us routine curiosity. Today I am an avid reader and I take particular delight in providing good reads for friends who are over ninety years old. There are still a few writers who can get me moving toward the dictionary or thesaurus — which became my constant companions in university and beyond, once I had no one to spite by not looking things up. So, although "Look it up" was much disdained by me in my childhood, I get it now.

Looking back — and we all have twenty-twenty hindsight — how much more helpful would it have been if my mom had dropped whatever she was doing and took the time to say, "Let's look it up together." I think I would have loved sitting on her lap, or beside her, with a dictionary when I was little, and the two of us finding the answer together. Then I might have associated new words and reading in general with love and affection, and be glad that someone was actually interested in helping me find the answer to my question. But it wasn't done in those days, as parents were too busy working hard to put food on the table; they were neither playmates nor friends to their children.

Here we are, a good fifty years later, and it's hard to think of kids today going to their parents for help in looking up anything. They have all now become so adept at finding information on their computers and cell phones. In fact, as grandparents, we are the ones going to them for advice on how to look things up. It seems I got caught in that in-between generation where both my parents and now my kids shake their heads and say, "Oh, for heaven's sake, look it up!"

4

Next to me, I love you best

My mom was one of the most giving people I ever knew. She showed love through her actions, as most moms do, but she was especially kind to her friends and family when they needed a helping hand — like with visits to the hospital, cards for a special occasion, a phone call to celebrate or commiserate, a meal delivered or an invite to dinner. She was altogether a kind, caring human being.

So, it came as a bit of a surprise one day when, in considering someone who hadn't been in touch for a while, she said to me, "Never forget. Next to me, I love you best." What was the message in that revelation? Did she mean, don't give so much that there is nothing left for yourself? Save your energy for those who will appreciate it? Don't expect that just because you are a natural giver you will get anything back? Or, as I always said when I worked in the not-for-profit and volunteer sector, "Never confuse giving with getting," especially when your own resources are incredibly low.

People will tell you that the best way to feel better yourself is to find someone else in worse circumstances and do something to help them. Really? How does that make any of us feel better?

Where does self-care come in? When is it time to look after me? Maybe that's what my mom meant all those years ago when she put it so succinctly.

Women are especially giving and nurturing since it is in our DNA. But a dear friend of mine said something to me the other day that really resonated. She said, "A *no* to you is a yes to me." At the time I felt bad that I was unwell and therefore, not able to celebrate her birthday with her. She said, "Don't look at it as letting me down. Look at it as saying no to me with no guilt, in order to take care of yourself." Wise words indeed.

Maybe this is the equivalent of putting our own oxygen mask on first to be ready to help others. It certainly makes me think back to the day my mom uttered that expression of hers, "Next to me, I love you best." If others can think that way, then maybe we should all pay proper attention to self-care long before we bottom out.

5

Everything was butter-side down

This was how our mom defined a day when nothing goes right from beginning to end. Everyone has a day like that now and again. You forgot the dog was still out last night and there he is half frozen at the back doorstep in the morning. You left the garage door open and the raccoons came in for a buffet supper, leaving the remains all over the garage floor. You didn't fill the gas tank and now the light is on and, oh yes, there is a snowstorm outside your door and the drive to work will be horrendous.

We all know that if toast falls on the floor and lands on its unbuttered dry side, it might be salvageable, as per the three-second rule, but not if the same toast lands butter-side down. That's just gross and reminds you how the kitchen floor is long overdue for a scrubbing. Ever try getting that butter off the floor? Well, the only thing worse is having an egg slip out of your hand and land *splat*, or having that jar of honey that was perched just on the edge of the shelf shatter as it hits the tiles, oozing stickiness everywhere.

I am reminded of the time our dog ate an entire brisket that had been left to cool on the kitchen counter. We waited a few days to see when said brisket would make its reappearance, and when it did, the dog was lying in his crate early in the morning and couldn't get out. Walls, cupboards, even the white carpet as far away as the front hall, were now all redecorated in an indescribable brisket shade. That was a butter-side-down kind of day.

Or you've been at work for a few hours when you glance down and realize you are wearing one brown shoe and one navy blue. Has anyone else noticed? Oh, well, if they ask, you will just say you have another pair at home just like them. We can usually cope with one misadventure, but a string of missed calls, or an individual announcing "Back in five minutes" and never returning, or ordering the wrong thing in a restaurant, or finding the grocery store sold out of chicken or miscalculating the distance in your rearview mirror while parking and bumping into the car behind you . . . can sometimes be too much.

It's a butter-side-down kind of day. Would that the saying could make everything better or put it all into perspective. But it's easier said than done. We've all had days like that. Never mind, tomorrow will be a whole new day and I, for one, plan to have cereal instead of toast.

6

Oh, you know, a little of this and a little of that!

Yes, but exactly how much of this and how much of that? I asked my mother, who was used to tossing recipes together. Being somewhat more of a control freak, I needed *specific* amounts and quantities that I could write down and then carefully follow.

What I learned over the years is that a little of this and a little of that was more than a style of cooking and baking. It was a recipe for life.

The first time I served her carrot *tzimmes* (tzimmished in Yiddish means mixed up), a dish at my holiday table, Mom asked "Did you parboil these carrots? They seem a little tough." My response was, "Did you tell me to parboil the carrots?" "But of course," she replied. "They taste better if they are softened first. You must always parboil them." Was this her way of telling me, *you have to live life to learn how to best live it?* Or was I joining a secret society of cooks who didn't give you all the ingredients or the right order in the right quantities?

There's the old joke about an amazing cook who, when asked, shares her recipes but always leaves something out so that no one will ever be able to replicate it as well as she made it! It took me many trials and errors with carrot tzimmes until I got it right.

It took years of holiday dinners and me thinking, this just isn't the same. Now, what might be missing?

The control freak in me was always screaming, *get all the details from her before it is too late*. The problem with cooking — and with life — is that some people are just good at it and it is so often what in Yiddish is called a *shittarein*. "A little of this, a little of that and, oh by the way I don't remember *exactly* how much I put in, but when you taste it, you will know."

How I wish my mother were still alive today. There are so many more questions I have about how she navigated her way through life, but sadly it is too late for that. I imagine having conversations with her about so many things, but her responses might always remain a mystery.

All I can think of is what she would say: "You will know. Taste it and you will see." I guess some recipes just have to be tasted, and you have to trust your gut instincts. I think that is where our true inheritance comes from, or maybe we just improvise and in so doing, stumble on the right recipe after all. Much in life is about trial and error.

7

Hanging out our teeth together

What do you do when you have a command performance that you don't actually want to attend? You know, the kind where your spouse has a meeting or a commitment where you are required to be present as the supportive partner. Your job is to go along to the event and smile, but sometimes it is such an effort as you really would rather not be there. As my mom used to say, she did not feel like "hanging out her teeth." Not that she had false teeth, but better that she did and could therefore send them along on their own for the evening.

Hanging out one's teeth was what one did at cocktail parties with people one barely knew and could tolerate even less. My folks were very social people and when they did laugh, it was the genuine thing. But it had to be in response to something witty, intelligent and bright . . . just like we, their offspring, were expected to be.

I remember falling asleep while lying on my bedroom floor with one ear pressed to the crack of the door, directly above the carpet. I used to love listening to the hilarity in the living room and sniffing the cigarette smoke that would filter under the door of my bedroom. Everyone smoked back in those days. As a youngster, I would invariably find a reason to come out in my Dalmatian feet-pajamas claiming I couldn't sleep, while both my parents and I knew full well that what I really wanted was to see what all their laughter was about. After being introduced around I would always go back to bed, reassured that it was grown-up stuff and nothing warranting my own participation. Besides, as soon as I was introduced, the conversation would lag. "Go back to bed, kid." I got the message.

Hanging out one's teeth was really about doing the right thing, and not about genuine happiness. There were lots of opportunities for the real thing . . . and then there were the obligations.

I was sharing this saying with my cousin one day and next thing I knew, she launched into a story about how she woke up in bed one night and felt something biting her leg. She reached down, and there found her husband's false teeth. How they got there was anyone's guess, but that gave a whole new slant on hanging out one's teeth that was really deserving of genuine laughter. Her husband, meantime, was fast asleep with his head on the pillow, so his teeth were out partying without his even knowing.

The message in all of this is to always be our most genuine selves. If we find ourselves in a situation requiring "hanging out our teeth," it really isn't worth being there at all . . . unless we are sound asleep in bed with someone whose teeth can hang out all by themselves. We need to learn to not take ourselves so seriously, and to laugh as often as possible. Life is just too short to have to attend too many command performances.

8

You can't make a silk purse out of a sow's ear

It was important to my mom that we align our expectations with reality. Of course she never told us that directly but more often through her wonderful expressions. One that I had never really thought about before came to mind: *You can't make a silk purse out of a sow's ear.* It didn't have quite the bite of some of her other cautionary missives like *don't cry over spilt milk*, and it definitely wasn't *some day you'll be sorry*, which we were warned on days when our behaviour had been particularly bad. It also wasn't *you'll put me in an institution* or *I'll send you to reform school*, both of which were intended to strike fear into the hearts of her offspring.

I think what my mom was trying to say was, "Lower your expectations and you'll never be disappointed." I guess she had known a few disappointments in her day too. And how can anyone not? It is our human experience to be regularly disappointed. It's how we cope with that disappointment that shapes us as human beings. My mom was clearly trying to teach me something, but I don't remember what it was.

A dear friend of mine has a habit of reminding me that my expectations of other people are in general way too high. Guess where I got that from? My mom always had super-high expectations of everyone (see chapter 4, "Next to me, I love you best"), and I guess I do too. My friend reminds me, "Expect the worst, hope for the best, and just be happy with what you get." She must have gotten that from her own mom.

My mom's version was *you can't make a silk purse out of a sow's ear*. Whenever you find you are disappointed in people, it may be the time to remember this. When our own kids disappoint, this expression rings especially true. Why haven't they learned the lessons we taught them? My father-in-law maintains that children are not adults until they are in their forties.

When other people disappoint, perhaps it's because our expectations are too high. You can't change the way people are and perhaps that was my mom's intended message. I certainly grew up in an environment where you didn't want to disappoint your parents. How could I do that? How could I achieve such a poor grade in my math test? It would reflect badly on them. How could I dress in anything but my best clothes when going out? (But change the minute I got home.) I was always very conscious of not wanting to disappoint. How times have changed, though, and with all the love we have lavished on the next generation, they do not feel any need to not disappoint. Jeans are good enough to wear to dinner. A T-shirt with a tear? No matter. Miss an important occasion? Oh, well. But maybe that's a good thing. Maybe I'm wrong, or maybe it's time to just let it go and stop trying to make a silk purse out of a sow's ear.

I think my mom was trying to say that some things just can't be fixed, as some people are who they are and will never be who you want them to be. Life has disappointments, and that's the way it is. Right up there with things you cannot change.

I still hear my mother's sigh and feel her resigned frustration. In today's vernacular, *it is what it is*. I guess I will just have to — as the kids say — deal with it.

9

A bad beginning is a good ending

When my golf shot goes completely astray on the first of eighteen holes, I console myself with my mom's words of long ago: "A bad beginning is a good ending." Maybe this was her way of saying, "Hang in there; it won't be all bad. Life has some redeeming features even if there will be trying times ahead. Don't get discouraged at the first sign of adversity. Never give up. Persevere. Keep trying; you'll get there. Anything worth doing at all is worth struggling for."

When I wanted to go home from camp within an hour of arriving, I was too miserable to pay any attention to her lessons. And on the first day of a job in which I was so disheartened and wanted to quit, I remembered these words of hers.

How could these words have helped so many times in my life? I was perhaps the most reticent camper, the most reticent traveller, the most reticent *away-from-home* student. Certainly, the first time I tried anything, I usually hated it.

As I grew older, these words finally crept into my consciousness along with the realization that my mom didn't always practise what she preached. Case in point: a forty-eight-hour stint in some holiday place where she was to work as a maid and change beds all summer. Her friends and family got together and bought her a lovely watch for a going-away present. She lasted not two days there before she hightailed it for home. Maybe her subsequent advice was born of regrets that she didn't stick it out — although those words alone used to make me cringe.

When the camp director heard how homesick I was and how badly I wanted to go home, he, who was supposed to have all this empathy and insight into handling eight-year-olds, announced that if I was good and didn't mention being homesick all week, he would come and sit at our dining-hall table. He certainly had a high opinion of himself, and now I liked him even less than the camp itself. The art director tried to draw a picture that was supposed to remind me of my wallpaper at home. It didn't, but what eight-year-old can articulate that it was little bunches of leaves on the bedroom wall, not the whole frigging tree? At least he tried. He really did.

What helped me was finding another little eight-year-old girl who was just as homesick as I was. Misery loves company and misery loves miserable company best of all. Together we commiserated and we got through it all. A decade after that summer camp experience, I was still reticent to leave home for university. University life was a challenge and seemed so foreign. I was not ready to be there but I eventually got my water wings and managed to ditch the horrible roommate I found cavorting around on my bed with her boyfriend one Sunday evening after I returned from a visit home.

First jobs and first dates do have a habit of sorting themselves out, one way or the other, if we hang in. My mom had good advice to give but, as I said, she didn't always follow it. I remember the story of her first time in court presenting a case before the judge. She argued brilliantly — so she was told after the fact — and briskly left the courtroom only to walk into the men's room. At first she didn't realize what had happened, but then, when she came out of the stall she encountered many colleagues, all male, standing guard at the door, saying, "Don't worry Miss Disler, we were making sure no one else went in." Talk about having your back. We always need people like that in our lives.

With her Californian perspective of the world, my sister always says, "Trust in the universe, and the universe will provide. The right job/house/partner/inspiration (substitute whatever word suits for the moment) will come along at the right time with the right qualities." Or, as I always say, "Feel the fear and then do it anyway." Those are more modern versions of "a bad beginning is a good ending," I am sure. A prime example of a bad beginning becoming a good ending is that our mom went on to have a brilliant law career despite that embarrassing visit to the men's room. And, as she always told us kids, she went on to marry my dad, who she claimed was one in a million, and that alone was worth everything.

As for bad beginnings, I did not get the marriage thing right the first time around (although we did have a wonderful daughter together). Then I met a fabulous guy when I was in my forties and, after being on my own for sixteen years, I could well appreciate the kind, gentle soul he is. We are now heading happily into our nineteenth year of marriage, so there may just be something to that saying after all.

10

Fleeing the Cossacks... abandoning everything

My dad's family found themselves in a tight jam with the Russian Army. The local recruiter wanted my grandfather and his eldest son to enlist voluntarily, or else the recruiter would come back and take them by force. Not knowing what to do, my grandfather told my grandmother to gather up their three boys and two daughters and bring with them only what they could carry. Meanwhile, at midnight on the far side of town, my grandfather waited for them with a cart. They would never see their home in Pruzhene again. Travelling as far away as they could, they came upon an abandoned farm in a town called Malech. There they found fields to work and an abandoned home. I was told this was not uncommon in the late 1800s in that part of Poland called Byelorussia — or Belarus today. This land that went back and forth between Poland and Russia was referred to as White Russia or Free Russia. The Cossacks were fond of harassing the locals, and particularly the Jewish population. The menfolk were constantly on the alert lest they be conscripted into the army without warning.

In Pruzhene my grandfather had owned his own granary and a store from which he distributed dry goods. Fleeing in the middle of the night was never part of his plans but that radically and suddenly changed. As my uncle told it, once the family was safely on someone else's land, they had to locate the storage boxes where food and clothing, winter coats and tools were often kept by previous owners. So they tapped everywhere on the ground out in the fields until they heard the *thunk* of the underground bins. Those supplies of potatoes, grain and other food stuffs would get them through their first winter on the farm.

In the spring, they planted crops so as to have food the next year. So began their time in Malech, where they remained until they left for Canada. There weren't any more details in my uncle's story; it was told very matter-of-factly while we were eating *latkes* — potato pancakes — in his kitchen one Chanukah. When I realized that this was my own history, I started paying closer attention. This was where my Uncle Herschel had worked all day in the fields. This was where my Aunt Sophie was so scared by the crows, bigger than she was herself at age six, that she did not manage to deliver her brother's lunch. Poor Herschel. Poor Sophie.

At some later date, my grandfather, and the elder of two daughters and the oldest of three boys. travelled to the New World. They did not speak English but knew of relatives who ran a business trading with the Indigenous peoples in Ontario. My uncle said the only things he could say when peddling items on his father's pushcart were, "Can I show you what I have? It will only take a moment" and "I can get it for you tomorrow." Just like that, they were in business. They taught themselves English, they learned how to provide what the locals needed, and some years later my grandfather and my uncle opened a clothing store, called Zacks and Son. Where was the oldest daughter in all this? She wanted to finish high school but was needed at home to cook for the men. I think her plan was to get out of Dodge as fast as possible, but that is a story for another time. She would continue to do the books for the business and run the household until my grandmother arrived.

Eventually, my grandfather sent for his family little by little as he earned the fare needed for each one to come over by ship. Next to come to Canada was my aunt Sophie and then the following year my father arrived. My grandmother would not leave her youngest son, who was not well, so she stayed behind with him hoping he would get better and they could travel together. My father, all alone and at the age of twelve, travelled by train, then by ship to Liverpool, England. From there he proceeded on to Saint John, New Brunswick, then to Montreal and, finally, by train, to his destination in Ontario — all the way from Poland. He too knew no English. Yiddish, Russian, German and Polish, yes. English, no. Imagine a twelve-year-old (who didn't know anything about this new country) waiting patiently at the train station for twenty-four hours to eventually be directed to his family.

Nowadays we wouldn't even send our kids downtown on a bus by themselves, let alone to North America on a ship. How times have changed!

How does one start high school with no English? I never learned those details. I only know that my dad did five years of high school in three and left for university and medical school shortly thereafter. Of course, there were stipulations. My grandfather wanted him kept far away from some gambling friends of his. They were going to the University of Toronto, therefore my dad had to go to Queen's University in Kingston, Ontario. Sheer determination and a healthy dose of guilt were probably driving my father. His family had a lot invested in getting one of their children through university, so he had better not disappoint. Hmm, I detect a family theme here.

I can't imagine, at age twelve, saying goodbye to my mother and sibling back in the Old Country and heading off on such an adventure, but survival was a pretty good driving force. Maybe that was the origin of his cautionary words, "Don't just sit there. Read a book!" It was thus driven into us kids from an early age that education was everything and, without it, we would be nothing. It all makes sense, given that my dad's family was literally driven out of their home, driven to survive, and driven right across the ocean to where my grandfather drove a pushcart. And our family legacy is all about being driven. It is exhausting.

11

On a bicycle built for two

How did a Washington lawyer end up in Canada? The details were never made one hundred percent clear. Probably because our mom was keen to hide her true age, or who knows what else. The story goes that my dad had come to Boston after the war, after he had served as an officer in the armed forces up in Canada's frozen north where, he told us, he had to chop through ice each morning to get water to shave with. Troops were being trained in temperatures similar to those on the Russian front, in the event they would eventually be heading there. Following his years of service, he attended a six-month refresher course at Harvard Medical School before returning to his home in Ontario to start his medical practice.

Our mom had been working as a lawyer for some time and was in Boston. A cousin, also a friend of my father's family, suggested to her a blind date with a young doctor from Canada. They met at a baseball game. No one recalls who won the game between the New York Yankees and the Boston Red Sox at Fenway Park, but clearly it was a home run for those two young professionals.

Mom was single, as were all the men coming back from the war. Dad, too, was returning to civilian life single. One ballgame was enough for him to know he would come back to Boston to date our mom.

After they had been dating for a while, he presented her with a charm to add to her bracelet. It was a miniature bicycle built for two. As my mother put it, she knew from that moment that this sweet, young Canadian was *the one*. Of course, at the time the song "On a Bicycle Built for Two" was all the rage.

Looking back, it seems very romantic, even all these years later. Together they would build a wonderful life. To marry my father, my mother came north from the U.S.A. to what she must have considered the backwoods of Canada. There is a tale of how they got stuck in traffic in the Sumner Tunnel under Boston Harbour and almost didn't make it to their own wedding. As my mother always told us, "A bad beginning is a good ending." And so it was — twenty-nine years of marriage on that bicycle built for two. It was a wonderful ride. Good thing my dad never suggested they actually go for a ride on a real bicycle. Did I mention that my mom never once rode a bike in her life? Never mind, she had plenty of good qualities and, even though she couldn't ride a bike, my dad must have known, too, how to make the best of it all.

12

Smile and the world smiles with you. Cry and you cry alone

Why is it that everyone else's life is always so wonderful? Our mom used to say, "I ran into Mrs. Smiley-Face in the grocery store and everything is always so marvelous with her and her family." It wasn't that mom begrudged anyone else their happiness (or was it?). It was because she wondered how no one else experienced sadness, tragedy or struggles. Everyone seemed to be fine. Or were they?

I know that I am a very open person. You don't have to be my closest friend for me to get into a serious or heavy discussion. You only have to be interested, compatible and sympathetic. And maybe we all have radar and an innate sixth sense when it comes to trusting and sharing our deepest, darkest secrets.

Certainly, the timing and place of interaction may have something to do with it. Social graces or emotional intelligence help clue us in as to those people we can trust and those we can't. We wouldn't want to confide something that is truly hurtful or troubling us to someone who might use it against us, or worse, share it with someone else indiscreetly.

I wonder if this goes back to not realizing that happiness and support are something that should be shared and spread, whereas sadness and hurt are something we take as personal failure and therefore try to keep from ever seeing the light of day.

The expression, *no one knows what goes on behind closed doors*, has always been true. It is behind these doors that people can let their hair down and truly be themselves. Another such expression, *never judge someone unless you've walked a mile in their shoes*, could be its corollary.

Who we trust and what we share is always a matter of personal choice and of judging that our secret will be safe and respected with a certain someone and not with another. Perhaps the grocery store, or the local charity meeting, or the water-cooler at work are not the best time or place for sharing important confidences.

And the truth is that while we have our angst and anguish, everyone else has theirs too. Sometimes it is too painful or too close to home to share something, while other times we wonder who really cares about our problems when they have so many of their own.

That gives rise to the question of how genuine we all are, and with whom we reveal our most honest selves. After all, everyone keeps certain things to themselves.

Next time someone smiles at me and declares all seventy-two of their children are top of their class, have a new scholarship, discovered a cure for cancer, won an all-important race or published a bestseller, I plan to take this claim with a giant grain of salt. Everyone has what in Yiddish is called *tsouris*, or grief.

It's part of being human to suffer. It's not that everyone else has a perfect life, but remembering the old adage, *smile and the world smiles with you, cry and you cry alone*, has always been, and may always be, true.

13

The White Lie

When I was three, I noticed that all of our neighbours had beautiful lights on their trees a few weeks before Christmas. Every evening, as it got dark outside, I would run to our living-room window and stare out at the wonderful multi-coloured lights and exclaim, ooh and ahh. What a treat it was, and how magical. It wasn't much of a stretch then to understand why, a few days after this discovery, I marched along our street to the far end of the block and began unscrewing the bulbs fixed on the lower branches of one of our neighbour's bushes. I brought as many of them as I could carry home to my mom and announced that now we could have our own lights. Not understanding that we were Jewish and, therefore, no matter how many pretty coloured lights I absconded with, we would never be having a tree, I was somewhat disappointed to be marched back to the neighbour to apologize and return the said lights. But little did I know how secretly delighted my mom was with my escapade.

 I was a bit of a rabble-rouser and, as I got older, I learned that my mother found my antics hilarious, as she felt she could never be really truthful about how she really felt regarding some people. I never learned the art of tact and diplomacy as a child, which is really one of the joys of being a child to begin with. But it was reassuring, as I grew older, to know that my mom was counting on me to be the person she herself would love to have been, and therefore secretly delighted in some of the things I got up to. This included saying things from my crib like, "Are you here, again?" to a frequent visitor. Turns out that was how my mom really felt too. Oh, the joys of having no filter at all. To be young and so painfully honest!

So what happens between the time we are two and three and say what is really on our minds, and the time we are old enough to understand tact and diplomacy or even the subtle art of the white lie? My mother, of course, had mastered the art long before I met her. You just never said those very words that you would love to utter!

Then there were the times when you deliberately told a white lie. I never understood why it was called a white lie. Was it that the white knight was always better? Why not a purple lie? Or a pink lie? Or even a green or brown lie, which, if you were colour blind, would be so much harder to detect?

For me, the favourite white lie of my mother's (which has worked on three husbands so far, her one and my two!) was when she would go shopping and purchase three different sweaters she liked, even though she knew that was excessive. Taking them home, she would put two of them away in her closet, and wear only one of them. If my dad asked if she was wearing a new sweater, her answer would be, "Yes, I bought it today. Do you like it?" Then, when she wore one of the other ones later on, if my dad asked if it was new, she could honestly answer, "No, it's not new. I've had it for ages." That reply was right up there with, "This old thing?" The white lie, useful for diplomacy although not strictly the truth.

Now, in this day and age of political correctness and equality, one might question why a wife or husband would have to fudge disclosing a purchase. Those of us who have been around the block a few times know that there is honesty, and then there is a slight alteration of the truth. Sometimes keeping peace at home is worth the price of such a small sacrifice.

14

You be the bigger person

Growing up, I would hear this and think, *how can I do that? What? How?* I am always going to be the little sister. There were only two of us siblings after all. So, whenever I wanted to stay up late or have a privilege that my sister already enjoyed, I was told, "She gets to do that because she is older. She gets to do it because she is bigger." How was that fair?

It took almost a lifetime to understand what our mom was trying to teach us. When friends would disappoint me by going off skiing without inviting me and I would suggest giving them the cold shoulder, out would come, "Never mind, you be the bigger person." When there was a slight or an injustice, I was told, "You be the bigger person." What my mom was trying to say, or so I assume now in my sophisticated adulthood, which eventually reveals all childhood mysteries, was "Rise above it. Be the better person. Don't stoop to their level. Aspire to something greater, nobler." More becoming of a Boston Brahman perhaps? Cheeky kid. My mom came from a family that was poor as church mice — or perhaps synagogue mice, as the case might be, so where did these lofty sayings come from? It's not like she had access to the Lowells or the Cabots or any of the Mayflower first families of the Boston elite. Living at the end of the Boston runway in Winthrop, Massachusetts, could hardly be a claim to anything other than the need for both my grandparents to strive to eke out a decent living.

Somewhere along the way, by reading and through life experience, my mom came to understand a whole lot more than she would have acquired simply at home. Law school perhaps, or debate society? Maybe. Hanging around with judges, clerks and other lawyers in Washington, D.C., gave my mom a pretty good idea there was a certain way to behave, and thus to rise above. And that she did through marrying my father, a young doctor from small-town Ontario.

So it was that we offspring were expected to behave better and to heed her wise words. I never understood the benefit of being the bigger person. Maybe it was her polite way of saying, "Suck it up, as it's not going to change. You can't change people, so make this into something you can live with by quietly holding loftier ideals yourself."

To this day I remember these words. When someone has treated me poorly, in my opinion at least, I try very hard to be the bigger person. Sometimes I confess that wanting revenge and retribution in the "Just you wait, 'enry 'iggins" * style, is much more comforting. But then I think, ah, what would my mother say? I'm sure she's watching from somewhere on high — all four foot seven inches of her — where she continues to be the bigger person, busily forgiving and forgetting so many of humanity's foibles, ones we'll probably meet all over again in the hereafter. Maybe, if there truly is such a thing as reincarnation, I will come back as five foot eleven, and then I can be the bigger person at last.

* "Just you Wait," *My Fair Lady*, 1956. Lyrics by Alan Jay Lerner and Frederick Loewe.

15

Comfortable in one's own skin

My dad's form of relaxation after working all week was to play golf, or at the very least, hit golf balls in the backyard — practice balls that had holes in them so they never left the yard itself. He would bring out a piece of carpet and set up his own driving range. We would collect the balls and bring them back to him. What could be better?

I'm sure many spouses decide that if they are not going to be a golf widow every weekend, they had better learn to play golf themselves. I was lucky because I started playing golf at age twelve, but my advice is to never take golf lessons from your parent. Terrible idea, a recipe for disaster.

My mom was willing to try golf in the hope that she would get to spend more time with my dad. But the mosquitoes had other ideas. She bought herself all the gear, the clothing, the clubs, but it seemed that the mosquitoes liked my mom a whole lot better than she liked playing golf. In fairness, she did like to put on some Jean Naté cologne every morning, so what smart mosquito was likely to resist?

Off she would go to the golf course where, try as she might to get herself into the game, she spent most of the time swatting away at mosquitoes. Over the years, as my dad headed off to play golf, my mom invariably found something else to do with her time, like reading newspapers or books, or checking in with us kids, or working on her various committees and community pursuits. Can't say I blame her.

No matter how late my dad worked, and he did work long hours, after coming home for a fifteen-minute dinner — which was always interrupted by calls from the answering service — my mom was quite content to see him off and then settle down to watch *Perry Mason*, *Checkmate* and other television shows of that era. Sometimes I would sneak out of bed and come in to join her. She would let me curl up next to her, both of us pretending I had gone back to bed. It never dawned on me that she might have been lonely for some company. And here I thought I was getting away with something.

Nevertheless, my first takeaway was to learn to golf young. I still golf to this day, not that I am any better now than I was when I first started, but I can join my husband for a game or play in a ladies' league, and still hold my own.

Not my mom. She decided she was quite happy sitting by the pool when she, my dad and another couple went on vacation. The three golfers would head off for a day on the course, and she would simply read or go off to explore the town. I always admired that about her. She didn't need to follow the crowd, but rather had such a good sense of self that she was fine being on her own. That was my second and more important takeaway: Be comfortable in your own skin.

My dad once told me, when we were discussing what I would do after university, "It's nice to have someone in your life, but never need that someone. Have your own career, your own interests, and always be able to stand on your own two feet." Not only was he a man ahead of his time, I can therefore well understand why he fell in love with my very independent mom. I guess that was part of the magic of their marriage, or maybe she provided the role model he admired best.

16

It all ends up in a parfait glass

My mom was an amazing hostess. She could cook and bake, and she was a marvellous entertainer. We grew up with hordes of people regularly at our dinner table. There were holidays with family, professional gatherings, committee meetings and impromptu get-togethers for coffee. When we moved to Ottawa, the nation's capital, there were ambassadors and charitable heads sitting at our table, as well as university professors and dignitaries. However, while all looked calm on the outside, my mother was a complete wreck from worrying. Would dinner be good enough? Did she remember everything, or would something be left in the oven and only discovered after dessert?

Inevitably, there would be a last-minute pre-dinner meltdown when, oblivious to all the hard work, I would pop into the kitchen to see what was what. There was my mother up to her eyeballs in pots, pans and mixing bowls, wishing she had a helper elf to run along after her and clean up. Then there was the cake that wouldn't rise, the Jell-O that wouldn't gel, the whipped cream that wouldn't whip . . . and all hell was breaking loose. It would never be good enough. "Go get the parfait glasses," those tall, narrow dessert glasses with short stems, and out they would come. This was always the backup plan! My sister and I used to joke that some day we would write a recipe book dedicated to our mom called, *It All Ends Up in a Parfait Glass*. Some of our mom's best concoctions ended up there, and we would all laugh when someone would ask for the recipe. Mom would say, "Oh, this is just something I threw together," and she wasn't kidding.

Her guiding principle in life was to make the best of everything. No matter what went wrong, her advice to us was always, "Oh well, make the best of it." And that was really what she was trying to do with the parfait-glass adventures. The mashed-up cake would go in along with the Jell-O, the fruit and the whipped topping with a little chocolate sauce, and, *voilà*, dessert. There's a lesson about not throwing the baby out with the bathwater, because the end result was always better than the original cake. It was her version of, "When life gives you lemons, make lemonade."

All I know is that particular dessert always seemed like a masterpiece to me. After everyone had gone home, my mom would admit that it turned out okay after all. And we could then let out our collective breath.

17

Sweet sixteen

The year leading up to my sixteenth birthday was a tough one. My dad fell ill early in the New Year. First he thought it was a cold, then the flu, and a few weeks later he collapsed on his way to the hospital to visit his patients. No one could figure out what was wrong with him. Back then, in the late 1960s, there was so much that was not known in medicine that is easily treatable today. Turns out he had pancreatitis. He had recently treated a case of this in the father of a classmate of mine and the patient was back on his feet within three weeks. Too bad no one listened to what they thought were merely the ramblings and hallucinations of my sick dad as he tried to instruct the doctors on how best to treat him. It was a very difficult time for my mom and an uncertain one for me. I would call home from the high-school's office phone each lunchtime to ask how he was doing while thinking, *what if he isn't alive?*

After many weeks in hospital, my dad did start to improve. Then his gall bladder became involved too, but, while still weak and much lighter than he had been previously, he was able to come home to recover. He was weepy when I came in from school each day to visit him in his room as he lay in bed. Nothing like a good health scare to make you appreciate what you have and to make you emotional and grateful for even the smallest blessings. I think we all recognize this as we get older.

That same spring, we were each living on our last nerve. Dad seemed to be well on his way to getting better by May, so we planned to take a drive down to my sister's college and pick up her belongings, as she would now be doing a junior year abroad. Partway back, on the return trip, Dad became quite ill again and in pain while we were at a roadside motel.

We quickly found the nearest airport and got him on a flight to Toronto, where he was rushed into the hospital for surgery. The three Zacks women then drove home alone. Dad would be okay but he would need to have his gall bladder removed.

On my sixteenth birthday, while he was recovering, I took a bus to Toronto to visit him for the day. My mom was already staying there with him. I then came home by bus and was met by my sister. To me it seemed an interesting way to spend one's birthday. My plan had been to head off to visit my best friend after stopping at home. As I left our house dressed in shorts, my sister asked if I was really going "dressed like that." Ah, the lessons from our mom had already sunk in. Now I got to thinking, *what's wrong with what I am wearing?*

So it wasn't a complete shock to find all of my friends jumping out from their various hiding places once I got to my friend's house. "Surprise!" they exploded with youthful exuberance. And they were all dressed in jackets and ties or in party dresses. Imagine that happening today. At the time I was so touched that I could barely speak. I was not expecting anything special for my sixteenth birthday, but my friend and her mom had organized this party for me so this birthday would not go totally unrecognized.

I was thrilled to be celebrating but sad that my parents had so much to deal with that they could not celebrate the occasion too.

The cake was spectacular and had little tokens, toys and coins in waxed paper concealed among its layers of chocolate and vanilla. I don't remember a single present I received but I am sure there were many. The one thing I have never forgotten is the kindness and care shown to me that evening, and just how special this friend and her mom made me feel. This was a true gesture of friendship and community at its finest, and I still get emotional thinking back on that day even so many years later.

It was a very sweet sixteen, in spite of my dad's illness. And having my dad around for another eight years was the best gift of all.

18

Happy Birthday, Harvey!

Today would be my mom's one hundred-and-sixth birthday had she lived past ninety-four. At least she may have been ninety-four, being someone who made a lifelong secret of her age, to the point where even her younger brothers — by five years each — were no longer sure how old their older sister actually was. And yet she liked celebrating these landmark events.

Always there was a birthday cake, usually from Woolworth's, as they truly were the best bakers of birthday cakes in our town. There were always candles, and we gathered in the dining room for singing and the giving of presents. Not that the candles were ever an accurate reflection of our ages, instead usually seven of them for good luck. Never being the exact number, my mom could thus keep her lifelong secret.

My mom never acknowledged that she was the same age as — or might have been, in fact, six months older — than my dad. There were never any ages mentioned. I remember when, with glee, my daughter announced in the doctor's office that she finally knew how old Nana was, after presenting her grandmother's health card inscribed with her birth date. I smiled benignly and said, "You only think you know."

Fact was, back in the war years when all the men were gone and working women were carrying the economy, people tended to marry later. No woman wanted to be seen as older than her husband, hence the fabrication of an age younger than that of my dad. What it meant was that in the olden days when you asked for a driver's licence in Canada, but were born in the United States, everyone just took your word for it that you were the age you declared. *Voilà* a driver's licence. There were no social insurance numbers back then, so ditto for that process, too.

What was fascinating for my husband and me was that when we finally went to my mother's birthplace to ask for her birth certificate, we were told, "Sorry, the hospital burnt down and those records were lost." When we finally found my mother's file one town hall away, her birth date was listed as one year, her marriage license stated another, the marriage certificate a different one, and yet another appeared on her birth certificate. So it remains a mystery never to be solved.

Because she always insisted that she was years younger than she really was, she had to act years younger — and so had friends of all ages, older, younger and much, much younger. Smart move. Thus, when some of her friends began dying, she had many others spread over other generations.

Birthday celebrations were probably therefore a bit traumatic for my mom. Especially her own. What if someone ever found out the truth? I know we never did. For her so called ninetieth, friends gathered at the retirement residence library to honour her. But was it really her ninetieth?

As we all got older, we stopped worrying about her age and just focused on the celebration. There was a time when my mom picked up my own daughter's birthday cake for me. As a single mom, I had little time between career and the day-to-day existence of running a household and making sure I was at all command performances, be they dance, piano or meet-the-teacher night. If my mom wanted to get the cake, fine by me. What she neglected to do was check to see what was written on the cake, which she admitted to me when she turned up at the table exhausted. The cake inscription read, *Happy Birthday, Harvey*. Wrong kid. Wrong cake. So back she went to the store during rush hour, struggling through traffic to make it back to our place in time for dinner.

It wasn't the first time this happened, either. She would mutter, "Oh, cripes," or "I checked the cake and I was livid." I still smile to this day remembering all the trouble she used to go to.

So, Mom on your special day, I am thinking of you with love and fond memories. I think of all the effort you made to show how much you cared for us, and how funny your escapades were both to honour those of us who readily divulged our ages and to hide your own. We always joked about how we would have to put a question mark on your tombstone where the birth date should go. Talk about taking secrets to one's grave.

So happy 106th, Mom. Or is it 103rd, or 107th . . . ? We will never actually know.

19

Good grammar, good grief

My mother was a stickler for good grammar and proper use of the right adverb and adjective, and no dangling participles, please. She was like a warden with a bad prisoner when we would come home from summer camp using expressions like ya, ya, or ya know, or any sentence that began with the word like. "Like, like, like," she would mimic us. "Where did you learn to talk like that?" she would demand.

I shudder to think what she would say to today's youth, and to others who are not so young, who seem to start every sentence with phrases like I mean or to be honest with you, along with many "And yahs," as if this were a complete sentence. Is it hip or cool to speak like this? The apple does not fall far from the tree, and I find myself wondering how these expressions get started.

I'm sure my mom is rolling over in her grave, or rolling her eyes from on high. Where do they come from? Why would anything come out of anyone's mouth that was not what they meant to say? It's as if the speaker is pausing to gather their thoughts out loud, at everyone else's expense. If you have nothing definite to say, then don't. If you don't know where you are going with your answer, just pause and figure it out.

A particular pet peeve of mine is parallel sentence structure, or the lack thereof. Seems *none* of this is taught in school these days. Emphasis on grammar is about as common as cursive writing and understanding the basic principles of arithmetic. Notice that *none* and *is* are both singular? *None* and *is* together are correct. How many times on the nightly news is the sin of bad grammar committed? It seems that now that we have our computers do almost everything, we have forgotten our basic arithmetic and the rules of good grammar. Even the computer itself will replace one's use of the verb *practise* — doing something over and over to get it right — for the noun *practice*. In fact, I am fighting with my computer right now as it keeps putting a c where I want the s to be.

I wonder what my mom would say about the expression *to be honest with you*. Would she think this means that everything else you have to say is a lie, except when it's prefaced by this very worn out introduction?

We were raised in a home where understanding the nuances of the English language was not only expected, but was raised to an art form of articulation. Woe betide anyone who did not use the proper tense, sentence structure, and such.

Any wonder that one of us two siblings became a communicator by profession and the other a psychologist? We were both driven towards our professions, so to speak. In today's irritating vernacular I could say, "I mean, to be honest with you, how could we be anything but? So, yah!"

20

Laughter through tears, or tears of laughter

Funerals are not a laughing matter . . . unless they are. Let me explain. My cousin Bertha passed away. Cousin Bertha was my dad's cousin first (actually my dad's first cousin) and then my own cousin second. I'm still not sure if this made her my second cousin or if we were also first cousins, but maybe once removed because of marriage. Putting that aside, the day for my older cousin Bertha's funeral arrived and it was very sad. She had been misdiagnosed and then succumbed to cancer far too early. Dying in your seventies, even thirty years ago, was still too young. None of this is a laughing matter. However, the funeral was a different story.

I was driving there with my mother, who was a dear friend of Cousin Bert. They regularly hung out together, as kids say today. They would go out for Chinese food and Bertha would always lament that the soup wasn't hot enough. Poor Bertha. All she really wanted was a bowl of hot soup. Before the service itself we were due to meet my Aunt Pearl and my Aunt Minnie at the funeral home. My mom and I arrived a bit early, went in and sat down in the chapel, to await the service. The chapel soon filled up with family and friends, and Aunt Pearl joined us. Then, right before the service was about to begin, Aunt Minnie, who was always a bit of a ditz, came running in breathlessly.

We asked her why she was huffing and puffing, and here is the story she told us. Seems that Minnie arrived at the funeral home parking lot early, but then saw a procession leaving for the cemetery. She rushed over to the last departing car and said, "You've got to take me with you!" I'm sure the people in the car wondered who Minnie was and why she was commandeering a back seat in their car, but since the procession was moving quickly, they had no choice but to let her in.

Minnie squished herself into the back seat, and off they headed to the cemetery. Flustered and wanting to say something, halfway into the ride Aunt Minnie exclaimed, "Isn't it too bad about Bertha?" At which point the driver turned around and exclaimed, "Bertha? Who's Bertha? We are burying Seymour." Apparently, in her haste not to miss the service, Aunt Minnie had jumped the gun and joined a procession from the funeral right before Bertha's. Business was booming at that funeral home that day, with people dying to get in.

Horrified on realizing her mistake, Aunt Minnie blurted out, "You have to let me out. Stop the car." By then they were way out of the city, on a dirt road. As Minnie became increasingly panicked and insistent that she be let out, the driver pulled over, in mid-funeral procession, stopped the car amid traffic, and my aunt promptly exited their vehicle somewhere in the middle of nowhere.

As my mom, Aunt Pearl, and I were still sitting waiting for the funeral to begin, we asked Minnie how she got herself back to the funeral home. She told us that she had hitchhiked back, and that is why she came rushing in at the last minute. Picture this eighty-something woman standing with her thumb out at the side of the road. I asked her who had given her a lift. She said she didn't know but she demanded that they bring her all the way to the funeral home, which, thankfully, they did. She was obviously getting this carjacking business down to a science.

On hearing her story, the three of us started laughing uncontrollably. In fact, we laughed so hard we cried. We then tried to stifle our bursts of hilarity as the service began, but with no luck. With shoulders heaving and tears streaming down our faces, we presented quite a sight of uncontrolled emotion. And then two of Bertha's friends sitting right in front of us, on hearing us sobbing and seeing the tears on our faces, turned around to comfort us, said, "Yes, isn't it so sad about Bertha," which set us off into hysterics all over again.

Needless to say, this was the funniest funeral I ever attended. Not bad enough that we were stifling tears of laughter all the way through the service itself, but at the shiva (the seven days of mourning that follow the burial) I told the story and left everyone there in hysterics too. So I think Bertha would have enjoyed her own funeral. She would have laughed along with the rest of us. She was a good sort and loved a good laugh, just as she had done on meeting her new son-in-law's family for the very first time. After they hosted a dinner they asked her as she was leaving to open up her purse so they could see how much of their silver she had stolen. She had howled then too.

Thirty years later, when wanting to share fond memories of her mom with her, I remind Cousin Wendy of that funeral story and we crack up all over again.

No disrespect, cousin Bertha. You probably deserved a more dignified send off. But the tears were genuine — genuine hysterics.

And every time we order soup in a Chinese restaurant, we think of you fondly. As my mom would say for years after, in any restaurant where the soup was served hot enough, "Poor Bertha, she would have loved this."

21

Sweet legacy

My dad passed away when I was twenty-four so I never really knew him when I was an adult, only when I was a youngster, a teenager and a young adult. Lest we think we pick up idiosyncrasies from just one parent, and although I had my dad in my life for a relatively short time, he nevertheless had a huge impact on my growing-up years.

I definitely inherited his sweet tooth. He would come down to breakfast in the morning and slather raspberry jam on his rye bread. Never toasted. As I was staring down at my own bowl of oatmeal, I might have said, "Hey, would you like some bread with your raspberry jam?" Such is my sense of humour, which I probably inherited from him too.

Occasionally, he would go to the convenience store and bring home a paper bag full of candy bars, including Oh Henry, Burnt Almond, Sweet Marie, and Jersey Milk. He would then store the bag on a shelf in a den cupboard, alongside some liquor, nuts and a nutcracker. Though he visited the cupboard only on Saturdays, we all knew the candy bar shelf was intended for all of us, so we would go and nibble on pieces of chocolate whenever we felt like it. Pretty cool. And guess who still keeps a stash of chocolate in the dining-room cupboard? I guess I inherited my dad's chocolate gene.

There are other things about my father that I remember, like the time I came home and, having just discovered skiing, begged him for a pair of skis of my own. Back in the day, these skis were measured to the height of your wrist held above your head. They had cable bindings that wrapped around the ski boot (secured with laces) and poles that had baskets on the bottom. No such thing as buckle boots, moulded boot or step-in bindings back then. Ski brakes? No, you chased down the hill after your runaway ski.

There was such effort involved in getting your skis on that, by the time you got all your gear on, you had already burnt a lot of calories. While my older sister was deep into books and school clubs, I was always yearning to ski. I would spend hours in front of our black-and-white television watching Jean Claude Killy ski the Swiss French Alps, and I would move my feet together across the carpet in parallel fashion, as if skiing alongside him.

When the time came to ask for some skis, my dad's answer was one I could have predicted. "When you get your grades up on your next report card, maybe we will consider getting you a pair." In my logical fashion, I pointed out that the next report card would not be until March and by then the winter would be over. I went off to bed disheartened and was totally stunned when, in my breakfast bowl the next day, I found a handwritten note from my dad saying that when he got home from the office that afternoon, we would go looking for skis. My heart soared . . . and he kept his word. What had changed his mind overnight? Maybe my mother? Behind every good man is a woman? I didn't question it, I was just so thrilled. I think maybe it was the fact that my dad had skied during his own youth and he might have been secretly pleased that I wanted to follow in his boot prints. Whatever the reason, I still ski to this day.

My dad, Louis Zacks, with his girls (ages 4 and 7) on our street in Peterborough, Ontario, winter 1957.

22

Keeping house

Many working moms today employ nannies and no one thinks anything of it. A nanny is a necessary part of survival for two working parents with a houseful of kids. When I was growing up, it was not so common to have a nanny, but there were a few households that employed what were then called housekeepers. This was especially true in the Jewish community, as many of the men were merchants in the downtown area and needed their wives to help run their stores. (Some stores, of course, were run by women who needed their husbands to help.) My dad was just starting his medical practice so my mom worked in his office. To practise law, she would have to take the Canadian bar exams, which would have meant returning to school. We kids were still young. We didn't have daycare back then. We had a housekeeper, Mrs. C., or, as we called her, DW, short for Dean of Women.

We never questioned her role in our household. My mom was always there when we came home for lunch. In those days lunch-break was an hour and a half and no one stayed at school. After lunch, until 6:30, my mom worked in my dad's office. Someone had to be home to look after us from the end of the school day up till dinner time. That someone was Mrs. C., who also did laundry, cleaned the house and cooked for us.

The only problem anyone ever noticed was that Mrs. C. had a speech impediment, and more than one grandparent, family friend or interfering busybody occasionally opined that we would end up speaking like she did, with her obvious inability to pronounce certain words correctly due to an unrepaired cleft palette from birth. She was also hearing-impaired. We heard a rumour that a stove had once blown up in her face, but there was no actual evidence to support this theory.

Despite those challenges, Mrs. C. became the backbone of our home. She was a mainstay in our kitchen, and a baker of wonderful pies, brownies and cookies, and we loved her like one of the family.

DW was older than both our parents by a few years. She kept a clean house, quite a feat, as her two feet were shod in red, high-heeled shoes. Thursday afternoon and every other Sunday were Mrs. C.'s days off. While present, she would play the piano without any sheet music and would read the paper daily cover-to-cover before my parents got home. When they were busy with volunteering or working in the evenings, Mrs. C. was always there to keep us in line.

She had been a hockey player in Nova Scotia and once played goalie in a women's league. I guess that was how my sister and I both learned to skate. Because Mrs. C. was hearing-impaired, half of the mischief we two kids got up to went unnoticed by her. Instead, she would be watching TV, reading lips with the sound off, of course, or watching a hockey game and doing her own play-by-play and yelling all kinds of advice from her coach's corner – while we would be nowhere to be found. Not that she was looking, mind you. She merely assumed we were either doing our homework or had already gone to bed. Instead, we'd sneak down the back stairs in a flash, lace up our skates and be out on our neighbour's backyard rink. This was at ten-thirty at night, and we were just ten and seven. We'd skate there for hours, thanks to DW having taught us, and would return home frozen, sneak back into bed where we were supposed to have been all along, and then pretend to sleep.

When we went to bed on the evenings my parents were at home, I, having just discovered books, would turn out my light when they switched off the television. After they passed by my door on the way to their room, I would put my light back on and Mrs. C. would emerge from her downstairs lair, knock on my door to see if I wanted anything, then assume her usual position in front of the TV. Long past midnight, she would check on me, still reading, ask me if I wanted anything, and head for bed herself. If it wasn't for our conspiracy, I doubt I ever would have developed my love affair with books.

There were times when I missed my parents, especially when they went off on a very occasional vacation together. Mrs. C. did her best by making all our favourite foods, but I still missed my folks. In case anyone wonders if their child will love the nanny more, the answer, in my experience, is no way. Mrs. C., however, was a constant, stabilizing presence. She gave us presents for holidays and birthdays and played football with me in the garage when it seemed like no one else had the time.

She also played with us on the driveway, and she never yelled at us for getting noisy and loud in the street. She would always call us to lick the icing bowl after baking a cake. When mad at me, she would yell at me to read a book. My sister was always holed up in her room, nose in a book anyway. When mad at my sister, she would yell at her to clean up her room, as mine was actually immaculate.

Mrs. C. went with us when we took a family trip to Toronto to skate on the huge rink at City Hall or when we met family friends with their kids in Niagara Falls. In short, she was considered family. She preferred to eat in the kitchen with us kids until we were "civilized" enough to join our parents in the dining room. But for her own birthday and all of ours, she was there with us in the dining room, smiling, and yet saying very little.

My dad and Mrs. C. maintained a nodding acquaintanceship. Yes, they lived in the same house, but I think each was terrified of the other and, because of communication issues (Dad being very soft spoken and Mrs. C. being hearing-impaired), the best they could do was maintain a nodding and smiling relationship. Picture two very polite people bowing in greeting to each other. As it turned out, both my sister and I are quite conversant in the English language and articulate enough for no one to guess that a primary influence in our lives could not pronounce our names — or many other words, for that matter. Maybe that's why we became good at languages in school. We spoke DW, or at least understood it from the beginning.

I was sixteen when we moved to another city. Taking Mrs. C. away with us would have meant separating her from her own daughter and her daughter's husband, their six children and their dog. Did I mention that we could never own a dog, as my mom feared that Mrs. C. would quit? (And yet, her grandchildren acquired their own fluffy white puppy, which they kept for years.) When moving day came, Mrs. C. moved into her very own apartment. Her husband had passed away some time before. Whenever I returned to visit her, she would make me all my favourites for breakfast — Red River Cereal, rye toast, freshly squeezed orange juice — and all her own favourite dishes: bacon and eggs. I didn't dare offend her so I ate every last bite. For the rest of the day I couldn't look at any more food.

Sadly, Mrs. C. died relatively young, in her seventies, from cancer. Even sadder was the fact that none of us in our family was able to attend her funeral, as we were then in Edmonton and my sister was away at school. We all should have been there for someone who was a huge part of the inner workings of our home and our lives, but it just wasn't possible.

Dean of Women, wherever you are, you were a very important part of our family. We have never forgotten you and, even more importantly, we haven't forgotten how you plugged in when our parents couldn't be there or what a huge impact you had on our growing-up years, making our house a place to feel safe and loved.

My sister, Ellie (12), Mrs. C, me (9), Mom (Adelyn) and Dad (Louis) in Niagara Falls, Canada, 1962.

23

Help is a four-letter word. Why?

It's a funny thing about women. We think we need to handle everything ourselves or else we are failures. Is it just me or do most women try to do too much? I'm sure there is a book on this theme. Maybe dozens. Why is it that help is considered by us to be a four-letter word? What would be so terrible if we asked for help from our husbands or partners, or even kids?

There I was in my kitchen, preparing meals for two households while our son and daughter-in-law waited for their preemie — born at just under two pounds — to come home to them from the hospital. My son was trying to work while his wife was spending all day at the neonatal intensive-care unit, so when they mentioned that food was going to be an issue by the time they both got home, of course I jumped to the rescue. Roast chicken? No problem. Brisket? On it. Potato pudding? Piece of cake. And they didn't actually ask me to cook for them. They didn't have to. When I suggested healthy, light, pre-made meals from the store, I was met with, "We don't like them." Okay then, what do normal people do in this situation? Do I actually think these adult offspring approaching — or already — forty are going to starve? Of course not. But still to the rescue I come.

All of this is beside the point. The real point was that there I was in a kitchen full of dirty pots and pans, mixing bowls and measuring cups and spoons, all of my own creation. I'd gotten smart and started sitting on a bar stool to prepare the food, but there is still a significant amount of up-and-down, back-and-forth to this cupboard, that drawer, the fridge, and the stove.

On this particular day, my husband came home early from work, probably thinking he would be able to relax. But I decided to ask him for help, and so by the time he stopped off at the grocery store to pick up milk and potatoes, picked up his clothes at the cleaners and joined me in a dog walk, there wasn't much of the day left. Still, I looked around at the disaster that was my kitchen and thought maybe I should ask for more help. And I did, although not directly, mind you. Instead I said, "I wonder if there was someone who would perhaps magically clear up these dishes for me? It sure would be a big help." What would be so wrong with coming right out and asking? After all, if you want to eat, cooking and cleaning are requirements for most adults. Yet, although I often mutter under my breath about meals being a participatory sport — and not just the eating of them — still I hesitated.

I've also been heard to mutter about my husband needing a passport to enter the kitchen, as it is a foreign country to him. All in good humour, of course, but really? Asking him to find something for me in the fridge is like asking him to make an expedition to the far reaches of Africa. I often have to tell him, "It is right there in front of you." I think this inability to find things in the fridge is common to many men, or is that politically incorrect?

I know that asking for help is hard for a lot of other women too. It shouldn't be. It should be a given. I am standing on my feet cooking for our offspring. Technically, they're his offspring, but

I acquired them in the merger and so consider them mine, nineteen years later. Some help cleaning up should be automatic, but if it isn't, asking for help should not be considered a sin. When I was growing up, my mom never asked me for help. I often offered, but she never said yes. Everything she did had to be perfect and for that there was only my type A mom. Of course, there was always the guilt that would be subtly, or not so subtly, laid on afterwards. But asking for help was unheard of.

Talk about women who do too much! Yet we think we must do it all: work outside the home, work inside the home, break the glass ceiling, as well as be domestic engineers, chief cooks, bottle washers, gardeners, snow removers, drivers, emergency babysitters. All I can say is thank goodness I don't celebrate Christmas. How people manage to decorate a house, inside and out, as well as shop for gifts, cater and cook for a feast, get it all on the table, only to have dirty dishes piled up to the ceiling for a week following... I can't imagine. Whew! Dodged that one. Oh wait, Passover is coming. Maybe it's time to ask for help. Hmm, I'll work on that.

24

Your eyes were bigger than your stomach

On the rare special occasion when our parents took my sister and me out to a restaurant, we would leave more on the plate than we ate. There were no kids' menus in those days, nor was sharing a plate between us looked on with favour by the establishment. Of course, we needed to be on our very best behaviour, and my dad would say, looking sadly at what we did not eat, "I guess your eyes were bigger than your stomach." Today I wonder what else we could learn from this expression.

During COVID-19, at the time of writing, everyone is learning to do with less, socializing less, eating out a lot less and certainly staying away from malls, stores, and any outdoor gatherings of large groups. No visits to indoor pools, museums, science centres or the theatre either. No movies or concerts. And, not knowing what the future will bring, we are certainly shopping less, except for basic food and other necessities. Our world has definitely changed, maybe forever.

I remarked to a friend that I kind of liked this getting back to the basics, entertaining and amusing ourselves and learning to live with a lot less. I also remarked that it was a perfect opportunity to avoid people we didn't really want to hang out our teeth with, but felt we had to out of some unseen or unknown expectation. I wonder on whose part?

Revealing to a friend that I was only keeping in touch with those who really mattered to me, and that I was finding the relief from all the stress of my normal existence so delightful, it made me wonder why I did all that stuff to begin with. Entertaining, visiting, command performances; who needs them? It was a relief simply being with my husband and my immediate family.

Did I miss all the running around and doing things? Not really. I was quite content to be at home, to stay cozy, and work on improving our living space so as to enhance our creature comforts. After saying all this to my friend, she remarked, "I gotta hand it to you. You always manage to find something good in every situation." Do I? And then I thought of my dad and his comment, "Your eyes were bigger than your stomach." Could it be that this was how we had begun to approach life, and were consuming far more goods and services than anyone really needed? Yes, they all look great and enticing, but why do we really need them? How big a television do we actually need? And how many do we need? I know people who have built-in theatres in their basements. I also have a friend who has no TV at all. COVID therefore provided a golden opportunity for me to take stock and get my priorities straight.

Really, how much does anyone need in order to just be happy? About the time I retired, I started going on builds with *Habitat for Humanity*—a wonderful not-for-profit organization that helps build homes for those living in very poor circumstances around the world — and I discovered that, amid all kinds of poverty the world over, people can be genuinely happy with very little. We were always told not to bring along anything that could not be shared, no lavish gifts or money to be given to the families whose homes we were building. Whether in Costa Rica or Vietnam, Macedonia or Nepal, and even in impoverished areas of Portugal, all of the families and individuals we met owned very little in the way of material things. But their existence always seemed rich in family life and laughter, in devotion to each other and to their community, and with a strong connection to their faith.

Nowhere we travelled was there huge evidence of consumer goods, the kind we ourselves have grown so dependent upon. Yes, they had cell phones and a refrigerator, and maybe a TV. The washers and dryers, if they had them at all, would be repossessed on a regular basis until they could afford to buy them again. They lived for each other, supporting each other, laughing and comforting one another, and taking delight in small pleasures.

Coming back home to Canada was always a rude awakening. It was a shock to realize how much we have here, how privileged we are, and how we take it for granted. Rather than seeing this epidemic as a time of deprivation, I prefer to see it as a chance to realize that our eyes may always be bigger than our stomachs, yet we can learn to develop an appetite for less and greater appreciation for what we happen to have in our lives right here at the moment.

25

Never close a door so tight you can't get your foot in it again

Get a teenager to do it while they still know everything. Funny comment that. The thing is that when we are young, we think we know everything. There's an old expression that goes, *the older I got, the smarter my parents became.* Many years ago, when I was discussing my job hunt with my (ex) father-in-law, his advice was to never close a door so tight you can't get your foot in it again. This was a rather important bit of wisdom coming from a man who was basically street smart. He had only stayed in school until Grade seven before he had to work on the family farm. Somehow life's best lessons have nothing to do with being book smart. As my mom used to say, "She went through university but did university go through her?" We can learn a lot from our elders, except when we are young and therefore know everything.

I never forgot my father-in-law's saying, and I think I learned a lot more from his down-to-earth wisdom. It's right up there with remembering to thank those who helped us on the way up, as we may surely see them on the way back down. Treat them with kindness and respect, and they will help us again and again.

The youth I know today don't seem to think much of old-fashioned networking, but it is so true that it is not what you know but who you know that matters. More importantly, it is who *they* know that will likely help someone like me get a job.

Even under those dire circumstances when you would really like to hurl some choice words at an employer who has let you go for whatever reason, it never hurts to send a thank-you note for the opportunity they provided you and the lessons you learned from them. As galling as it may seem while you are being helped to pack up your stuff and then walked out the door of the office, letting people go is as hard on the manager charged with the task as it is for those being dismissed.

I try to tell our offspring to be gracious, no matter what. You don't really know anyone until you've spent a day in their shoes. And what we see on the outside is not always a good reflection of what's going on inside.

My mom used to say, "She smiled at the world and the world smiled back at her." Or, another of her favourites, "You attract more flies with honey than with vinegar."

Hard as it may seem to be empathetic at times, it can make all the difference in how the world sees you, and in turn how you see the world. It's important to be kind to people all the time, but especially so when they have gone out of their way to help you.

When a young friend of mine was looking for a job in a very specific field, I wracked my brain to come up with every single person I could think of to help her. I would suggest contact after contact and explained how I knew them, how they could help, and what their connections were. Needless to say, when I heard back from said contacts that the same friend never got in touch with them, I was upset that she had never even bothered to open that particular door — never mind close it too tightly. What had I done wrong? I clearly meant well but didn't spell out the benefits clearly enough for her to feel inclined to call them.

Maybe she wanted to manage it all herself. Sometimes we want something for someone more than the person we are helping actually wants it for themselves. Sometimes it may seem intimidating to have so many connections that the person we are trying to help simply tunes out. Sometimes they may feel overwhelmed and defeated before they even begin. And, who knows, today's job searching may be all about connecting through job sites on the internet and not about personal contact.

We ourselves were always taught to go for the information interview to learn everything we could about the industry or field in which we were interested, where the gaps were, where the trends were heading, and what we ourselves might be able to offer. Has all this become passé? Am I out in left field? With all the technology today, are people not as important sources of information as they were when I myself was seeking employment? I still think it is people who make the decisions and can open doors for us, but I may be wrong. I'll let you know if the same friend lands herself a job without another human being involved.

26

One day you will

My mom must have had great expectations for us kids. She wanted us to have all the things she herself dreamed of but never could afford. Summer camp — which I hated and pleaded to come home from — or piano lessons for which practising was truly awful. As soon as the kitchen timer went off after ten minutes, I was, as they say, outta there! Swimming just struck fear into me. *Oh, please don't make me go.* Ballet, tap and baton were the way to learn proper deportment and grace. But not for me. And finally, in case we got bored, there were Hebrew lessons and Sunday school. My fondest memories of going to synagogue services were, of course, getting into mischief with my friends, including locking the stall doors in the ladies' room from the inside-out, and watching the other congregants who needed the restroom wriggle and curse in frustration. Many of my childhood sins were committed there in synagogue so I really was a holy terror.

But we were also introduced to the theatre, which I loved, and to skiing, skating and tennis, which I also liked. As for the rest, it was a matter of just getting it over with. What an ungrateful child I clearly was. And yet I was happiest of all playing the electric eye on our block, a game invented by my older sister, and much like hide-and-seek. When someone was caught, the finder would proclaim, "The electric eye is upon you." Climbing trees, playing baseball with the local kids, and riding our bikes on the street were the best form of entertainment. I was a kid who wanted to discover the world on my own terms, in my own neighbourhood, and I had no intention of ever growing up. My mom must have been so disappointed in me. She told me so often enough. Ah, well. I would blaze my own path.

One of my fondest memories was introducing a new-found beau to my parents at the dinner table. The two of us had been going out for a while before he came home with me from university. Very clearly, my parents did not approve. How the conversation turned to opera, I don't remember. Maybe something came on after the CBC radio news, which was a mainstay during dinner time. In response to my offhand comment that I would never get to like opera, my mother — convinced that I would surely come to my senses — said, "Oh, some day you will like opera, you'll see." To which the said boyfriend responded to her, sotto voce, "And some day you will play football!"

I thought that comment hilariously funny. The image of all four foot eleven, hundred and ten pounds of my continually shrinking mother — by then in her early sixties — playing football was just too funny to resist. I had never thought of responding in that way and found it so refreshing to put her words into context. Okay, it was actually rude, if you think about it, but that was not the point. My parents would continually try to impart life lessons to me and try to mould me into someone I just was not meant to be. Meanwhile, I would continually resist and deflect them where I could. Funny how memory of these things comes back to us when we are older. All those lessons about thanking people for dinner the day after, sending appropriate sympathy notes, remembering birthdays and special occasions, all that stuck with me, including being a good friend when someone was in need.

No, I never did grow to like opera. Yet there are plenty of other cultural pursuits I enjoy, so I like to think my parents would not believe me now to be a total failure.

And my mother never did learn to play football, so I guess we are somehow even.

27

Small-town kid meets big city

When I was growing up in small-town Ontario, we hardly ever locked our doors; only at night or if we were going away for a long period of time. Most of the time we were pretty easygoing about the safety of living in our neighbourhood. Fifty years later and here I am in a suburban big city; not quite a bedroom community, to be sure, but much quieter and so-called safer than living in the major metropolis right next to us. Until the break-in, that is. We were at work. It was an ordinary day. Until it wasn't. I got a call from our dog walker that our front door had been jimmied open in broad daylight and all manner of drawers were tossed open, contents spilled everywhere. Our dog, Smurf, gated in the kitchen, kept the thieves from encroaching on the main floor by barking continuously. The truth is that our beloved Wheaten Terrier just wanted the thieves to come play with him, and he would probably have licked them to death. "Come on in. Let me show you where the valuables lie. Over here is the treat cupboard. Want one?" Okay, a watchdog he wasn't. The jewellery they took had great sentimental value as some were gifts from friends, and some were handed down from my grandmother and mother.

We were so shaken by the experience that we installed cameras, for I wasn't yet ready to put in an alarm system. As the security company told me when I inquired, "Alarm systems are for those who have been properly traumatized. Trust us, cameras are actually better."

So we installed cameras. To what good, though? Could we sleep better at night? What smart criminal doesn't already know that if they pull a hoodie over their head, no one will know who they are, camera or not? Honestly, I could make a good criminal myself. Nevertheless, those cameras were installed. Nine years later we had reason to review the footage gathered from four different motion-activated cameras around the exterior of the house. On that particular occasion the crime was the misplacing of our garbage-can lid. A crime of high import indeed.

When I came home at the end of the day on the Tuesday in question, the garbage can was still there but the lid was off and away on its own adventure. But what good is a can without a lid? Pursuing the matter, I called the city administration offices and was told that if I had footage of the misdeed actually taking place, the City itself would replace the lid, or even the whole garbage can. Generous to be sure. It was then that I remembered our installed cameras, so I actually went through the entire footage of that day.

Very interesting, what we discovered. First, I had to call the company that had installed the cameras to get the code and password. Then I had to figure out how to find the precise day the lid disappeared and what time-span to check. I discovered that the garbage crew had arrived on their truck at 9:04. One of our favourite City workers grabbed the can, took off its lid, and emptied the bin itself. Then, because some of the garbage had stuck to the lid, he took said garbage lid, jumped onto the running board and they were off — along with our garbage-can lid.

I took pictures of the *crime* in progress from the security footage, then sent them on to the City, who promised they would look into it. I also noticed, from the same footage, a car in our driveway that should not have been there. We tried to zoom in on the licence plate, with no luck. We rewound the footage to the time the car arrived. The driver got out of his car, put on a pair of gloves, then a hooded jacket, and went to open his trunk for some gear. This man must be our burglar! He next headed to our neighbours' gate, so we figured maybe they had rented out their basement, as we noticed someone new hovering in their backyard. "Well, I'm going to tell those neighbours that their guests can't park in our driveway," said my irate husband. Whereupon I said, "Let's call the police. He's obviously now breaking into our place."

When said burglar could not get in through the gate, he pulled out a cell phone. After a short chat, he headed to the other side of our house and let himself in through the back gate. When next picked up by our backyard camera, there he was at our barbeque. Help, I'd forgotten that a repairman was due to come to service the barbeque. All this kerfuffle over a barbeque repairman. As my mom would exclaim, "Well, I never!"

It's nice to at least know that our house is secure even when we are not at home. In the meantime, we noticed — also on the camera footage — that someone has been leaving their blue bins on our driveway. That's okay, as I'm sure they just didn't get up early enough and therefore missed the pick-up. I'm not really that paranoid.

Which reminds me. We still have no lid for our garbage can and, one year later, the City is still looking into the issue. Meantime, garbage day is Tuesday. Maybe they will put the lid back then.

28

You can choose your friends but you can't choose your family

Never a truer statement has been made. I recently returned from a weekend in the U.S.A. with a lifelong friend, Pat — not her real name — whom I had met years ago through work. Her work eventually took her to the States, which was an excellent way to escape her dysfunctional family and be free to become who she really is. Why was her family so dysfunctional? Isn't everyone's in some way or another? I never knew the details, but I did know that with all of her successes she never felt validated by her family who in fact seemed to resent her moving away to take a better job. I also knew how distraught she was every time she came home or when something in the family happened that would upset her.

However, moving to a new city and starting over with no friends whatsoever is a daunting task. As with everything in her life, Pat had a strategy in mind as she set about meeting people — new people. She joined the local tennis club, learned to play golf, made friends at her new company and also on her travels.

She nevertheless missed the idea of family and flew home often enough, but it wasn't until a new neighbour, Marta, moved in that Pat finally had someone who needed her. Despite the thirty-plus years age difference, the two became fast friends. Pat had never married, although she doted on her nephews and nieces. Her neighbour, Marta, still in her early twenties, could never be her true self around her family, as well intentioned as they might have been.

Pat eventually became like a second mother to Marta. She possesses lots of sage advice — and until then had no one to pass it on to — and she had a special knack for relating to young people on an equal level, thus putting them instantly at ease and making them feel like co-conspirators.

I could sense the love in the room as the two of them bantered back and forth. How was your date? Will you see him again? Is he cute? It was the kind of relationship you would want with your own mom, if you could. And I can't count the number of *I love yous* that went back and forth between them during the weekend I was there.

If that isn't like creating your own family of love, I don't know a better example. When I left for home, the pair were busy planning how to get through a Thanksgiving command performance at Marta's folks' house, and Pat was planning *Friends-giving* for the day before. She has made a whole new family with her love and compassion and energy that no one back home has ever truly appreciated. Well, I had. And I miss her and admire her. She is truly an inspiration, making a life of meaning and love.

I learned a lot from that weekend visit. We can never change our family of origin, but we don't have to relive the negative. Instead we can have a whole do-over, and hang out with the people we wish were our family. So, it's never too late.

29

Plan B

Recently, my husband came home with an ink splotch on the breast pocket of his white shirt. There was no way this would be coming out at the cleaners, or in the wash using bleach. After thinking and thinking of how to make the stain vanish, other than making the whole shirt vanish into the garbage, or making it part of my painting attire, I thought of my mother. What would she have done?

My mom always had a plan B and she became most creative when she had a disaster to sort out. For instance, consider spilling something like pomegranate juice on something made of white jersey. Today we would simply go online and look it up to find a solution. Thus, when I got blackberry juice on a white shirt, I learned that pouring boiling water over the fabric stretched over a bowl will take it right out. Who would know that? Back in the day — as our kids say — there was no Dr. Google. Instead there might have been a long line of grandmothers who knew exactly what to do so that solutions got passed down from generation to generation, like an oral legacy.

What I recall is that one day my mom would be wearing a sweater that was entirely white, and the next day it was peach with blue flowers on it, thus matching her navy skirt perfectly. She was a master of making something very different from something ordinary, and very good at disguising a stain or an ink mark. Upon finding such a stain on her clothing, these not quite swear words would immediately follow, "Oh, cripes." No F bombs were used in that generation, and definitely not if you were raised in Boston and aspiring to move up in the world. Even in extreme moments, a curse would be something more like, "Oh, that b – i – zitch!" Always the lady.

There she would be, like a benevolent witch using a stick to stir her concocted brew in the cauldron, meaning laundry tub, full of some colour or another, and working her magic while waiting for the result.

Hours later, an entirely new item of clothing would emerge. How she managed to achieve this without turning the entire bathroom or kitchen the same colour as what she was tinting, I find amazing. In a discussion with the owner of my local craft store, we agreed that if I myself took on this task of banishing the ink stain, not only would my laundry room end up blue, so too would my clothes, the dog, and anything else that happened to be nearby. True, our first dog's name was Smurf so the blue might have been explainable, but this current one's name is Winnie, named after my mother's home town of Winthrop, Massachusetts. I have seen many breeds out and about in my neighbourhood, but none of them are actually blue.

So to me, all of this comes under the warning of very risky behaviour, and I have discovered, looking back, that risk-taking was what my mom did superbly. For who marries someone, then leaves her own family, friends and career to move to a new country far from a bustling, vibrant American city to a small Canadian town? Someone very much in love, is my guess.

Back, then, to my husband's shirt. Navy would likely be the only colour that would properly cover that ink stain. An easy decision, but finding the Tintex, which was always kept in our cupboard when I was growing up, was not as easy. Why not stencil some stars, or something else creative, on the pocket alongside the offending stain? Why risk the entire shirt? Good point. I sense a new trend in the making here: one-coloured shirt, patterned pocket. I'll let you know how it turns out.

And, if all else fails, we will go to plan B, acquiring a new shirt for me to paint in!

30

Putting your best foot forward . . . may have something to do with your footwear

The secret supports in one person's shoes, or, it takes a village of footpads to keep a person on their feet.

"Put your best foot forward," my mom used to say, though who knew what that meant? My thinking, when I was young, was it meant look your best, be on your best behaviour, be the best person you could be. Not that I knew how to do any of that, but smiling politely, saying "Thank you" and "Pleased to meet you" seemed to fit the bill. Hidden in there was the idea that we should always behave our best, despite not always feeling like doing our best. What if being okay was good enough? What was this need to be better than someone else? Why couldn't we just be ourselves and let everybody also be themselves?

Furthermore, how do you make your feet feel *better*?

After my mom passed away, I was left with all of her clothes and shoes. She used a cedar wardrobe that she had kept for years and years. I never knew everything she kept there, but it became mine after she moved to a seniors' residence in her later years (age about eighty-nine). There was no room in her new home for this cedar wardrobe, which had a lock and key, and so it moved into our basement. I never really looked inside it, but I knew there were some very nice outfits, a fur coat, and other odds and ends, like important papers. My mom has been gone twelve years now, and I am thinking it is finally time to empty it out. Lo and behold, what do I find in the bottom of said wardrobe but pairs and more pairs of shoes. Not just any shoes, but ones that have been specially altered to fit my mom's feet. She was always complaining how her feet were no good and she was always going to visit the podiatrist.

She had contemplated foot surgery many years previously but so many doctors warned her there was no guarantee she would feel any better after the surgery. It seemed some patients suffered more pain after their bunion surgery than they had before it. Nevertheless she would comment, "Look, there goes Betty Thompson running down George Street after her foot surgery" with a hint of envy and a wistful sigh.

Thinking I could now perhaps, at long last, discover the secret to *putting one's best foot forward*, I took a good look at her shoes. There was a soft cushiony insole and additional padding in special spots to protect her feet. The shoes also had been professionally stretched to accommodate the various deformities or nuances of her foot. I got to thinking that if her shoes had to be altered so she could wear them, then maybe there was a message here that would enable all of us to put our best feet forward. Perhaps custom-made footwear, like the way ski boots are fitted to form? Maybe with a little adjustment here and there, we could become our best selves. Or at least our feet could be their best, and if they were comfy in the world, then we could be too.

If women really want to be on an equal footing with men, how on earth are we ever supposed to achieve that while running around in high heels, forever concentrating on not falling over, while men wear flat sturdy shoes that enable them to have both feet firmly planted on the ground? What if men had to go to work in a tight skirt and high heels, just for a day? How would they be able to put their best foot forward — or would they even be able to walk? In this day and age, however, I suspect this whole thought process is politically incorrect.

There is putting your best foot forward metaphorically, putting your best foot forward in a podiatric sense, and making sure we are well grounded in order to risk putting any foot forward at all.

My mother-in-law has many maxims, but the one that comes to mind is, *right foot first*, which we are always exhorted to do when about to get on a plane. Does it really matter which foot goes first? I tried doing this with my carry-on and found that if you have a bag in your left hand, then the right foot is automatically positioned first. But if you carry the bag in your right hand, then it's the left that goes first. How is that likely to affect the pilot's ability to fly the plane? And what is the pilot wearing on his or her own feet? Is your right foot genuinely the best foot to put forward? Isn't it much more important which foot the pilot puts first? I'm just hoping it's the best one.

I have now decided that choosing which foot to put forward is not the issue. Nor is comfortable footwear either. I think what my mom meant was, get out there and be the best you can be. Perhaps it's not about the feet at all, but what is in your mind that matters. A positive attitude can probably overcome all superstitions, bunions, corns, and hammer-toes, and even enhance the pilot's ability to fly the plane.

I really must get rid of all those clothes in the cedar wardrobe, and footwear too. But looking at all the accommodations my mom had to make for her shoes to fit her at all makes me wonder if maybe the saying should be, *put your best shoe forward.*

31

Nothing is ever black or white . . . unless it is

Growing up, we were never allowed to have a dog (see chapter 22, "Keeping house"). "Some day you will have your own home and then you will have a dog," our mother would say. So guilty did she feel about denying us kids a dog when we were children that she insisted on buying my daughter and me one when I was in my forties. Smurf, so named by my daughter, was the light of our lives and lived to almost sixteen. His successor, Winnie, so named for my mother, who hailed from Winthrop, Massachusetts, came into our lives two years later.

It had been the kind of summer when the temperature rarely goes below thirty degrees. Sounds wonderful, but for our four-legged family member it was really hot to be wearing a fur coat all day. Thus the need for walks only after the sun goes down. So we walk early in the day, and then again for a short time midday, and finally one last walk at night. It was one such July evening when my husband, dog and I set off on our usual route. By the time we neared home, the sun was fully down, the moon was out and the crickets were off and chirping. So too were the other little creatures venturing out of their daytime hiding spots.

While we were enthralled watching a still-as-can-be rabbit, which we were sure Winnie was also contemplating, the dog was instead looking at a black-and-white one. Too late we realized it was actually a baby skunk, who was now protecting herself by doing what skunks are best known for, right into poor Winnie's face. Up close, not only does a skunk not smell like the road kill we often smell from afar, but Winnie could not get that smell rubbed off her face fast enough. Here was this poor dog trying to wipe her eyes, nose and mouth on the grass and against the curb all the way home, clearly in considerable distress. Meantime, we were planning our strategy for coping with this awful smell that was heading home with us.

"First," declared my husband, "she doesn't go inside the house."

"Right," I replied. Then I quickly googled what to do with a skunked dog. Fortunately, neither of my two dogs had ever been skunked before so I had plenty of never opened Skunk Out from dog one and unused Skunk Be Gone from dog two. At first, in my panic to get her cleaned up, I could not find either bottle, but Winnie was still busy wiping her face on the hedges and the deck out back.

Once I found it, I tried to catch Winnie, who was cavorting about all over the place. When we set off for our walk we had decided to run the sprinkler, so now not only was Winnie getting wet, but so were we. Wet dog is not great at the best of times, but wet skunked dog takes it to a whole new level.

Finally, we got a bucketful of soapy water and doused the poor dog like we were putting out a fire. That certainly got her attention. We would get her all soaped up ... and then she would slip through our hands and be off again on a tear. Poor thing had received the majority of the damage just under one eye. We were very careful to wash it out with lukewarm water, as instructed on Google. It also said to mix hydrogen peroxide — I was sure we had a bottle somewhere — with baking soda and dishwashing soap. Did we have enough of it? And would our dog blow up, as in the science experiment where baking soda is used to simulate a volcano?

My husband ran off to the drugstore to buy a large bottle of hydrogen peroxide. Turns out we only needed a little, so what we already had would suffice. Anyway, the drugstore was closed. No matter. We eventually got the sad, smelly, dejected creature all cleaned up, and she really didn't smell too bad by bedtime. "No, you cannot get up on our bed tonight. Just go to your crate."

Poor Winnie. This was really not her day. Talk about traumatized. Not only did she get sprayed by a creature she mistook for a rabbit, but now her parents didn't want her anywhere near them. There's a cause for childhood angst, for sure.

When we got home the next day, we could still smell skunk, so we repeated the whole process.

From that day on, when we are out walking, anything black and white gives Winnie pause. She definitely suffers from PTSD: post-traumatic skunk disorder. When a black- and-white dog recently approached her to say hi, she went ballistic, barking and going on the attack. I can't say I blame her. She even ignored a fuzzy toy skunk that a friend of ours gave her to play with, clearly fearful that it, too, was going to attack her. The whole episode was quite an experience. And we will be avoiding anything black and white for some time, I'm sure.

Meanwhile, I have been told that for the six months after a dog gets sprayed by a skunk, it will smell like skunk all over again every time it gets wet. Oh, goodie, I can't wait.

32

Don't shoot yourself in the foot!

Don't cut off your nose to spite your face. These words came from the woman who raised me and asked me on a regular basis if I wanted a nose job. Really? That one was pretty obvious. No, I did not want one. I like my nose. And it likes me just fine. But, *don't shoot yourself in the foot?* Ah, the hidden meaning behind all these body-part metaphors. Could it be that she was actually saying, "Don't sell yourself short"? (But, Mom, I have always been short!) Kidding aside, she meant that just because we all have our shortcomings, not everyone — including a future boss — needs to know them at an interview. Could she mean, *Get out of your own way?* The Buddhist version would be, *the path is clear, so don't throw rocks in your way.* Or did she mean, *the sky is the limit... Fly!* In other words, *Get out of your own way.*

There are times when we all sabotage our own efforts. We have doubts about our abilities and often say, "Who me?" when awarded an honour or receiving credit we surely couldn't possibly be good enough to deserve. Honestly, when I sit down to paint one of the photos I have taken on my travels, I remember these words, and those of Henry Ford, who once said, "If you think you can, or you think you can't, you're right."

So where do all these positive people come from? We all have met them. They are the can-do people who always say, "Yes," and not "I'll try." They don't even respond with, "No problem," giving you a sneaking suspicion there might be one. How do they get to be so positive? Certainly they didn't grow up in my household, where a lot of second-guessing always went on.

My mom had plenty of regrets, but then she was, after all, one of the Regret Sisters — Would've, Could've, Should've and Mom. She was right up there with the big three. I can't count how many times she uttered a regret, usually to do with something she did or said that she shouldn't have done or said. With us, there were lots of self-doubts and lots of conflicting messages. Who knew if she ever felt nervous getting up in front of a hundred or more women at Hadassah-WIZO events, or speaking at national conferences on public affairs issues or, for that matter, getting up in front of a jury and the judge in legal disputes during her early career? In her bar admission exam prep-class, which she taught in New England, there must have been many students who passed through her classroom.

Me? I was terrified of the Four Questions that the youngest would ask at the Passover seder, not to mention the paralyzing fear that would glue me, and my shaking knees, to my seat in school when impromptu speeches were called for. Five-minute speeches had me throwing up over the toilet bowl for weeks before the final competitions. And yet, somehow, in my own career, when I was asked to address a national conference or participate on a panel, I finally learned how to take the bullet out of my foot or, at least, get the butterflies to fly in formation. Maybe it was because I thought I knew what I was talking about, and therefore had the courage of my convictions.

One thing I learned from my mom as I got older was how to exhibit grace under pressure. Fake it 'til you make it. Paste that smile on your face until you feel like smiling, and get out there. I use this a lot now that I am retired and can climb back into my comfortable shell. Dinner parties don't terrify me the way they did my mom. Hey, if the guests don't like it, well, they didn't have to pay for it, they didn't have to prepare it, they don't have to wash dishes — and next time I invite them, they don't have to come.

When I sit down before a blank pad of watercolour paper and feel my confidence going right out the window as I try to figure out the parallax or the horizon, or how the heck I am going to paint that picture before me, I remember the little train that could. *I think I can, I think I can.* I vow to read that one to my grandkids early, so as to give them lots of positive reinforcement for their good qualities. And when I say to them, "You're smart. You're kind. Aren't you a love?" I mean it with all my heart because a kind word or two along the way in your growing-up years can mean so much in later life.

In my first public relations job, my boss told me the reason I was offered the position was because I was tenacious. At the time I didn't know if that was an insult or a compliment, but when I looked the word up, I thought, *yes, I am.* And I continue to be so to this day. My daughter also has inherited the ability to fight for what she believes in.

I guess the message from my mom, which she never actually articulated, was something like, *You have so much to offer. Get out there and do it. I believe in you. Now you believe in you, too.* And when my dad once told my mom that my sister was smart, but that I was the one to watch, I think he meant I would go places. I like to think I didn't disappoint him.

33

Looking like you just stepped out of a bandbox

Our parents thought it cute to have my sister and me dressed alike. We were not twins, in fact three years apart. But what could be better than two little girls in matching dresses? How much fun! Not if you are the younger one. You have about six years of wearing the same style of dress — three in your own and three more in your big sister's.

I wasn't so worried about what I was decked out in. I already knew that party dresses are not comfortable, especially when sitting in the back seat of a freezing-cold car. The heat never seemed to reach us back there; for the entire ride to Toronto we would shiver. How jealous we were of the children of my parents' friends who would meet up with us wherever we were going for the weekend, wearing corduroy pants and sweaters. We, however, always had to be dressed — as our mom would say — as if we had just stepped out of a bandbox. Whatever did that actually mean? We would grow up playing musical instruments, in my case badly, but that was not the point. We played in the school bands and wore band uniforms, complete with jacket and tie. Thank you, Dad, for teaching me how to tie a Windsor knot properly, as it's a skill I could never have lived without. It's true that in later years I felt proud I could tie one for any of my dates who hadn't quite mastered the hang of it. I guess wearing a tie was a kind of litmus test for determining who would make the grade when I brought them home. Imagine anyone putting on a tie to meet one's parents today. My dad was always dressed in a suit and tie, except when he was on the golf course. A dear friend even once asked if he slept in his suit and tie. No, but he did put his suit on over his pajamas to make middle-of-the-night house calls. Maybe his desire to be well dressed was part of his charm that swept our mother off her feet.

Dressing well was an absolute necessity, my mother insisted, she who once got up at five in the morning for a shopping trip to Montreal and put on one blue shoe and one brown. How could she ever live that one down? After all, you never know who you might bump into and, oh, the embarrassment! As she always warned, and as we were to learn in later years, the number of acquaintances you meet on any outing is directly related to how poorly you happen to be dressed. Remember Snow White and the Seven Dwarfs? In our house there was an eighth dwarf, Shlumpy! Wear your finest and you are likely to meet no one, but put on that ratty old pair of jeans and a comfy but worn-out sweatshirt to run to the store for just a moment, and there will be the entire community — or at least the ones by whom you don't want to be caught dead "looking like that."

Why all this emphasis on looking our best at all times? To this day, even as I am running out the door, I check our strategically placed full-length mirror to ensure I won't embarrass the Bureau, aka the Fashion Police, of which our mom was the Director General. She had style and class and an unerring sense of how to put outfits together with panache. She was always in demand to commentate fashion shows for her friends who owned clothing stores, which constituted a huge part of the commercial engine of our town's main street. She gravitated naturally to those women whose wardrobes were impeccably put together, and she learned the knack well. Or maybe she was simply born with an innate sense of which colours went together.

My cousin once told me that when our mom first came to meet my father's family, she was wearing a navy and green ensemble. In those days people actually said that "blue and green must never be seen," but that caveat didn't deter her from trying something new. That was her trademark. If there was something you shouldn't do, mustn't try, or wasn't done — by women especially — there would be mom setting a new trend.

There was a message in all of this, and it wasn't just look your best and you will feel your best. As with many of my mom's sayings, there was often more than one meaning and sometimes they are completely the opposite. Blaze your own trail and don't let other people determine who you are. Really? So why did we two sisters have to be dressed so perfectly? Well, you just never know who you may bump into.

My sister, to this day, will never fly home wearing a pair of jeans. In fact I am not sure she even owns a pair. The one good thing about being the second-born is that a lot of this stuff just rolls off you, and I always had absolutely no interest in looking my best. But that was then and this is now. And besides there is that mirror in the front hall. Did I mention it was my mother's? I half expect her to be looking back at me, saying, "You're wearing that?" Today — and especially having been through the pandemic — I think many of us are just happy to wake up again in the morning. Being at home, with all social life restricted, I have found that I don't miss dressing up smartly at all. Well, maybe just a little. Putting on our favourite clothes is usually so comforting. And, anyway, if we can't even go out, who's going to see us? It's good for us to get our priorities straight. But then there is still the mirror in the front hall. Maybe I should just slip out the rear door and go hang out in the backyard.

My sister, Ellie (6), Mom, and me (3) in 1956 in our backyard.

34

'Twas the week before Chanukah (during a pandemic)

Growing up, we always looked forward to our annual Festival of Lights. Our neighbourhood was predominantly Christian, so most everyone had their trees decorated, even the sixty-foot-tall ones (at least they seemed sixty feet to me). My sister would come and get me at around five in the afternoon and take me to our living-room window, where she would lift me up to see what was the most beautiful display of magical colours that my four-year-old eyes had ever seen. It was truly spectacular.

We did have our own traditions though, and one of them was eating latkes. Problem was that our mother was highly allergic to the skin of every fruit and vegetable: apples, pears, peaches and, yes, potatoes. This was the only time our dad was to be seen in the kitchen, wearing an apron over his suit and grating potatoes for those latkes. My mom may have been the ultimate cook and baker but, as you know, behind every good chef is a sous-chef. So there he was, grating those potatoes. I don't remember eating the latkes, but I do remember lighting the Chanukah candles every evening for eight days and opening presents on one night as well.

Fifty years later, here I am in my own kitchen the week before Chanukah, dreading the effort it will take to grate make an entire ten-pound bag of Yukon Golds with the help of that best invention ever, the food processor. Each year I reckon I have mastered the art of the latke. First I make the gluten-free ones for a friend, then the egg-free ones for the allergic family member, then, finally, the rest for my family and friends who will have no idea how long it takes for the smell of cooking oil to leave one's house, hair and clothes. It is truly a labour of love.

The oil has to be super hot, but not hot enough to burn. For if it isn't hot enough, the pancakes stick. If it's too hot, they become crispy outside but remain raw inside.

This time it is like the telling of the story of Chanukah all over again. I thought I had enough oil when I first looked at the bottle, but then I wasn't sure. Should I leave everything and run to the store for a fresh bottle of oil? As I got to a hundred latkes, with forty-four more to make, I began to wonder if the oil in that bottle would last. But it seemed every time I needed more oil, there was still enough, even though, at the very end I had to turn the bottle upside-down to squeeze out its last few drops. Sure enough, the oil lasted — to the extent that, when I checked later in the day, the remaining oil had leaked on to the counter (see chapter 33, "No good deed goes unpunished!"). Finally, all 144 latkes lay nestled on tons of paper towels to soak up all the oil.

When I was a kid, there was a regular commercial on television for cooking oil. Its makers extolled the virtues of their oil, and how, when you finished using it, the used oil could go back in the bottle, except for one tablespoon. Really? Not in my kitchen. There are now gobs and gobs of greasy paper towels (organic, of course) in my garbage. And all the latkes are now snug in the freezer, awaiting their delivery for what I assume will be our Zoom Chanukah.

It's still a magical time of year, with lots of good memories of Chanukahs past. So I think I will go wash my hair one more time. Happy Chanukah!

35

Monday comes the revolution!

What was this revolution that was proclaimed almost every weekend? Repenting for sins committed over the weekend itself? Over-indulging? In her later years, our mom was great company for trying out new restaurants: Vietnamese, Chinese, fish, pizza, and all manner of food we were technically not supposed to be eating in good Jewish homes. But what we did outside the house was open season, and it was always great fun going out to eat with her. She never let me pick up the tab, either. In fact, she and my dad had developed finely honed skills at grabbing the bill before anyone realized it had arrived. No amount of persuading her would work, and her promise of "You'll get it next time" would never be fulfilled. It was not allowed. Parents paid, and that was that.

No greater insult could be inflicted than to somehow outwit my parents when it came the time to pay. On their birthdays and special occasions specifically in their honour, even after years of me earning my own income, when the bill arrived, they managed to pick up the tab. Even long after both our parents were gone, whenever my sister and I would get together, a battle ensued over the cheque every time. It was a family tradition after all, and our duty was to continue with it.

But I digress. We were talking about Mondays and the revolution. No, my parents were not Communists and there were no Marxist leanings in our household. Socialist, maybe. Empathy definitely, community-minded and spirited for sure.

My mother was ahead of her time in that she mostly ate very healthy food, as I recall. Often, she would regale us with tales of some lunch or dinner where a companion at the table cut off every last scrap of fat from her meat, or wouldn't eat the skin on the chicken, and it seemed my mom felt very impressed by this. Unbeknownst to me, as such things were never discussed, my mom had been warned that she had high cholesterol. It was this, therefore, that drove her to eat yogurt and cottage cheese, salads and white chicken only. She was simply being careful. Since she lived well into her nineties, I can only assume it must have worked. However, whenever we got together, she would indulge heartily while saying she was getting fat as a pig, and that none of her clothes would fit her if she kept eating like this.

Recently, on seeing a photo of her Nana, my daughter remarked that she looked very tiny, and that she had never realized how petite Nana was. I guess, like the homes we grew up in, or that hill in the front yard or that tree that towered over us, we accorded our elders an authority and gravitas that made them seem bigger than they were when we were still so little. My daughter's remark struck me as funny since mom was just mom and she held all kinds of stature and status in our home — which also turns out to be much smaller seen through adult eyes. My mom seemed much smaller too as she got older.

Nevertheless, petite or not, our mother became pretty careful about her diet after finding out she had acquired a high cholesterol level as a result of genetics. I'm not particularly thrilled with such a legacy either. I cheat a lot, it's true, but I do exercise much more than my mom ever did. Just having a dog keeps me out walking many, many steps a day. Even so, these remembered words — *Monday comes the revolution* — have crossed my lips many times. Frankly, what good are weekends to you if not to cheat on your diet? Isn't it better to live a few years less and enjoy the things you love, like good food? Those are the words of my cousin who spends half her life on the treadmill. As for myself, I am always trying to stay ahead of the curve — or the bulge.

The thing I don't understand is how every ten years another five pounds manage to affix themselves to my body. It's not like this happens precisely on the decade; it's more like a sneak attack beginning three years into it. This process has been going on since I was in my thirties. And so, every decade I have fought to lose an additional five pounds from the decade before. How did my mom manage to do it? I guess every Monday was a reset. For how else did she stay so tiny?

I have no energy for making dinner tonight and, after eight days of Passover, I feel like sinking my teeth into something decadent. Ah, there's the doorbell now. The pizza has arrived. But, oh well, *Monday comes the revolution*, and, oh yeah, today is Monday. Well, there's always next Monday, so I guess the revolution can wait one more week.

36

"Don't worry, I'm fine, dear"

When are we grown up enough to know what is really going on? And why do parents feel they have to constantly protect us?

How often did I hear the words, "I'm fine, dear," after discovering to my horror that I had just opened the door of my mom's apartment and unwittingly bowled her over? How could I know she was right on the other side of the door? Yet, at eighty-eight she bounced right back up like the Energizer Bunny and insisted that, not only was she completely fine, she was accustomed by now to being flattened by an over-exuberant daughter knocking her flat on her back as an everyday occurrence. I, of course, felt mortified. Are you sure you're not hurt? Should we get the nurse to check you out? No, no, never been better. Ha!

Little did I know how often she had started falling over in her latter years. I remember one time returning from a vacation and phoning and phoning my mom's apartment, but there was no answer. Then when I reached my home, there was a message from her friend, Molly, telling me to call her. Sure enough, Molly told me the story of how my mom, in her usual gung-ho fashion, had gone charging ahead toward the bank on a none-too-even sidewalk, only to land head-first in a hole in the pavement.

Couldn't she just walk at a normal pace? Even with her walker, she was always running. "Not to worry," her ninety-five-year-old sidekick added, "She is just at the hospital, but it's nothing serious." Yikes.

There was the time I received a phone call while having my haircut. "This is TD Bank," said the message. "Can you please call us? It's about your mother." I called them right away and received a voice message: "Due to an unforeseen incident, the bank is now closed." *Great*, I thought. *My mom has been taken hostage in a bank robbery.* Should I let them keep her? My curiosity and concern of course got the better of me, and off I tore to the bank.

There were people gathered outside and boards being erected on the front of the building where the plate glass window used to be. I identified myself to the police and my mother's customer rep came running over to me, saying, "Your mother is fine. Don't worry." Seems my mom had taken to drive-through banking. Apparently, her car had leapt the curb and driven right into the building. Lucky the poor person withdrawing cash at the bank machine in front of it was not hurt. "Where is my mom?" I asked the police anxiously. "Don't worry," they said. "She is fine." (Were they also part of a conspiracy to protect offspring from their parents?) "The tow truck has just left with her car, and they were driving her home." "But what actually happened?" I asked. "We don't know, but you can probably reach her at home by now," was their reply.

Turns out there had been a small matter of a black-out, with my mom having no recollection of what happened. I think it was what they call a TIA, or mini stroke. "But are you hurt?" I demanded when I spoke to her at last. "No dear, I'm fine." Sure.

But the car had been totalled and my mom gave up driving that same instant.

Another time I arrived at the retirement residence to find her covered in black-and-blue bruises. What on earth had happened? She said she had no recollection of having a fall or banging herself. Had she been mistreated at this very elegant retirement home? When I asked my husband what could have happened, he very innocently suggested that she had probably just hurt herself rolling over in her sleep. Really? Rolling herself right on to the floor? I then asked the nurse, whom I had come to quite like, "Do you know what actually happened?" Her response was similarly vague, but she told me not to worry as she would keep an eye out for my mom. Little did I realize that my mom had sworn both my husband and the same nurse not to say a word to me. What was she afraid of? That I would put her in a retirement residence? She was already there! My husband would cite patient-doctor confidentiality and I would then remind him that she was not his patient.

It's mysterious, this keeping of things from adult children. I wish I had known the truth every time my mom uttered those "Don't worry, I'm fine dear" responses. I knew full well that she was *not* fine.

On another occasion, when she was still living in an apartment on her own, she called me up and asked if I had time to come over. "What's wrong?" I asked, a feeling of dread coming over me. "Oh, I stupidly tripped on the rug and now I can't lift my arm. Maybe I should be going to the hospital." I felt like asking, *You mean you can't drive yourself?* — as she had once done after falling down the subway stairs. On that occasion she had promptly picked herself up, hobbled back up the stairs and driven herself to the hospital with a broken leg. So progress was being made if she actually called for help this time. It turned out that she had dislocated her shoulder, requiring surgery!

On her way to Rochester to visit some good friends for the weekend, she once skidded on some spilled coffee in the airport and actually broke an arm. She carried on with the weekend visit, not saying a word, until Sunday night when she returned home and then took herself to the hospital. Either she had a very high tolerance for pain or she was stubborn as an ox. I'm thinking more likely she didn't want to worry anyone or interrupt the general plans.

There was another time she caught her heel on the uneven edge of the elevator. She then went ahead with a dinner party for eight, while in excruciating pain. Three days later, when she thought maybe she shouldn't travel with us to Boston by car, she convinced us to go ahead while she would catch a plane the following morning. But, instead of calling a taxi to the airport, she summoned an ambulance and was admitted to hospital for what ended up being neurosurgery on her spine, as vertebrae in her back had collapsed.

On moving day, my mother insisted she would be there to help us move into our new home. All was fine until late that night, after we were settled in but feeling exhausted, she went charging off out the door. There were no lights on the steps as yet, and as a result she missed the second and third steps, landing on her two front teeth, which then had to be replaced. Cracked beyond repair. Only the teeth, thankfully, that time. She never even told us that she needed to have them replaced!

At a family friend's house after the Passover seder, we were standing together at the top of the steps. "Hang on to me, Mom." But did she? No, she went barreling off, as was her style, fell face-first into my friends' garden, and I, big help that I was, fell right on top of her. There we were, both of us, faces-down in the mud. Classy guests, the pair of us.

Looking back, I am grateful for having had my mom around for so many years, as she seemed so bent on self-destruction. But little did I know just how often she was falling. The last incident was a broken hip while I was on a work trip to Vancouver. I dropped everything immediately and took a red-eye home. Even on the night before surgery, she insisted she was fine, although the pain meds she had been given left her delusional and asking why my dog had been walking around up on the ceiling.

I have to say, she was feisty to the end, and it was always "I'm fine, dear." Would that we all had the resilience to lie through our teeth — replaced or otherwise — the way she did, with a smile.

37

Rugelach reminiscences

The times I feel closest to my late mom are always related to the kitchen. The smells and sounds as I am following some of her recipes make me remember similar times in the kitchen with her, and the extremes to which she would go to make sure her recipes came out just right. I tried one today for rugelach. Every Jewish kid grows up loving this sweet croissant-like pastry filled with either raspberry, apricot, chocolate, or cinnamon and nuts. It's generally found on every celebration table and at every commemorative event, and therefore at most Jewish holidays. It is basically a mainstay in the cookie/nosh department.

I should have known it would not be as easy to make as the recipe indicated, even if it was a Norene Gilletz* favourite. The cream cheese turned out to be too soft, the margarine not hard enough, and where the heck had I stored the rolling pin? Rolling out dough using an oatmeal spurtle (don't even ask) is no substitute for a good old-fashioned rolling pin. There I was, up to my elbows and ankles in flour, trying to achieve the right consistency of dough. Finally it resembled a ball, so flattening it in the shape of a circle and then dividing it into the rugelach slices like pie pieces seemed easy enough. But how to get the sugar and cinnamon, chocolate and pistachios to stay inside the dough? That remains a mystery to me. My mom had probably learned all these secrets, or inherited them through her mom. For me it became trial and error.

Finally, all seemed ready for the oven and yet, over the next eighteen minutes, I had the distinct impression something was burning. "Oh, cripes!" my mother would have uttered in frustration. I had done it exactly as the recipe said, so why were the bottoms burnt? Come to think of it, the last batch of chocolate cookies I had made were similarly burnt.

Luckily, the grandkids don't care.

Once they hear "cookies!" from Bubby (their term for me), they climb into their car seats with speed. Yes, they can be bought — the kids that is, not the cookies. Although I also know lots of good places that sell rugelach, I can attest that I feel no connection to anyone or anything except the rugelach themselves when I buy them. The kitchen where I make them still connects me with my mom. What would she do with a batch of burnt cookies? Probably toss them out. Me? I scrape off the burnt bits and just carry on. Of course, I will try them again some time, but the good news is that, even though I was raised in my perfectionist mother's home, I long ago decided for myself what was good enough. For me, scraping off the bottoms is quite good enough. Besides, I'm watching my weight.

Another batch? Maybe, but not today. I have other things to do. It was nice to have my mom around for a bit.

---

* Norene Gilletz was a well known cooking maven originally from Winnipeg, Montreal and Toronto where she wrote or co-authored numerous cookbooks that have become mainstays in most Jewish kitchens.

38

High time for high tea

My mom always loved the idea of high tea. It was a very British, high-society custom that appealed to her Bostonian sense of style. Dressing up, having fancy-tea sandwiches, scones with jam and clotted cream, and a pot of tea — what could be more civilized? I can't remember when she first introduced me to high tea, but I have been hooked ever since. Tea was regularly served in our household as a finishing touch at the end of dinner. Not coffee, as they always drank that with milk, and dairy is not allowed after eating meat, according to kosher law.

The high tea episode is how I refer to the night before my daughter's bat mitzvah (rite of passage for twelve or thirteen-year-old Jewish girls). On that occasion, the out-of-town dinner guests were gathering at my mother's apartment. The caterer had made various levels of boxes covered with fancy tablecloths on which to place their exotic creations for the dinner. No parfait glasses needed here.

My daughter, who was so eager to do her bat mitzvah portion the next morning, was not feeling well. I too felt under the weather, probably caused by nerves. My aunt was recovering from an ailment, and another was suffering from Crohn's. Not subjects for dinner-table conversation, but in the background nonetheless.

The buffet dinner was lovely and about forty relatives and friends, mostly from out of town, were scattered around the apartment enjoying the feast. I myself was only able to manage a cup of tea. I took one sip of it and went running into the kitchen to ask my mother what on earth this disgusting brew actually was. She glanced around the kitchen and then asked one of the wait staff what they had served.

The answer was that they could not find the tea provided by the caterer and so had looked in my mother's cupboard, where they had found a purple bag containing tea bags. This they had brewed and were now serving to the guests. A horrified look crept over my mom's face. "Oh no," she exclaimed, "that's my laxative tea!" There weren't enough bathrooms to handle the traffic that evening.

By the next morning in temple when everyone's stomachs had settled and before services began, I told the rabbi the story of that tea. Towards the end of the service — which our daughter handled with great skill and confidence — the rabbi made a special announcement. He declared that there would be a luncheon at the conclusion of the service for the guests of our family, and a very special tea would be served.

High tea indeed! Mom would never be able to live that one down, and all of us who had been at dinner the night before had a good chuckle.

Our tradition of high tea continues. Whenever my husband and I go travelling, we seek out a new high tea. From Paris to Prince Edward Island, Bermuda to Charleston, South Carolina, my husband humours me in my desire to check out the local high teas. For my birthday a few years ago, I invited all of my friends to our home for a tea party. It was a salute to friendship and a way to honour them. There were the scones with clotted cream, the party sandwiches, the fruit and all manner of petit fours. There were also many different varieties of exotic teas. I'm happy to say not one of them was the same one served many years earlier that resulted in great laughter at the bat mitzvah service the next morning.

39

No good deed goes unpunished!

Nicely put, whoever coined the phrase. It certainly came to mind immediately as the brisket gravy ran down my apron on to my jeans and then continued down to my sneakers, to the point where even my socks were soaked and my shoes made squishing noises across my newly washed kitchen floor.

The brisket adventure began when our latest grandchild arrived three months early. She was much smaller than the three-pound brisket I was preparing for the new mom and dad so they would have food in their fridge when they finally returned home. After spending a week in hospital, much of the time with doctors trying to decide whether on not to take their little brisket out of the oven, they were both going to need sustenance. The decision was finally made, and our little granddaughter arrived. Thus the need to begin cooking, which is my response to most crises. What can I make? What can I bring? What can I deliver since, clearly, I myself have no role to play in the delivery of said baby? In general, how can I help?

With this pressing urge to do something, anything at all, I hit the grocery store followed, in short order, by the kitchen. It was after the brisket was cooked, sliced, cooled and ready to go into an already full fridge that I realized, after first tilting the pan one way and then another, that it was still not going to fit in the meat drawer. That's when the foil pan made a decision for itself, collapsing in my indecisive hands and sending all that gravy cascading.

Immediately, I thought of the last time this had happened to me. It was some forty-five years and one marriage ago, when I invited my then in-laws to our newly rented apartment to join us newlyweds for our first dinner with company. I had dutifully washed the kitchen floor with Lysol and was pulling out the roast and potatoes when the tinfoil pan collapsed. Roast and potatoes went spinning across my newly scrubbed, chemically fresh floor.

Even with my back turned to my in-laws, I could not disguise what had just happened. Nevertheless, I served that dinner after doing a cursory rinse of the main course. If anyone else tasted Lysol, as did I, no one said a word. Now, fast forward more than four decades later to another kitchen and another life. Maybe it was crisis-communication training that helped me see the funny side this second time. And maybe it was time to buy a proper roasting pan. All I know is that our prematurely born granddaughter's vital signs are good. She is stable and her mom and dad are learning to juggle their lives while running back and forth to the neonatal intensive-care unit in the middle of a worldwide pandemic. We grandparents, meanwhile, are pitching in as best we can. While new mom and dad are eating homemade brisket and chicken, salads and vegetables, we ordered ourselves pizza for dinner. I think most parents want to do the right thing by their kids. I know my own did, even if sometimes their intention was better than the outcome.

And, of course, when a well-meaning cooking marathon ends up on my floor, I think of my mom and her frequently saying "No good deed goes unpunished." To me it means that even though there might be a disaster in the kitchen, it's the good deed that really counts.

We have just received a very grateful thank-you message from our kids, with excellent reviews of my dinner. So I feel like I have been given a Michelin star. Then, again, I was doing what my mom taught me — to contribute where and when it's needed, or as my dad would say, "Don't just sit there, do something!" My shoes have never been cleaner and the soaked jeans are in the laundry. And, like they say, "It all comes out in the wash," anyway.

40

**Cross that bridge when you come to it . . . or,
Get out of the buggy, Becky; you're not there yet**

We all tend to worry about the future, especially when the present is not providing us with a whole lot of comfort. There's worrying, and then there is worrying to excess. In fact there is a psychological condition called free-floating anxiety, where if you are not worrying about one thing you're worrying about something else. I like to think I come by my worrying naturally. What if this happens? What if this happens and then something else happens? We can become so absorbed in worrying about the future that we forget about living in the present.

Such has been my own state of mind over the past few years, and probably even longer. As I get older, I realize I have less time ahead of me now (in which to worry) than behind me, so I have to worry double-time to get all that worrying in before I run out of time. Where did I get this trait? I have no idea. My mom was not a worrier, neither was my dad. They took everything one day at a time, or so it seemed to me. I'm sure my worrying has to do with not having a lot of control over my environment as a child, for we always had to behave as perfect little children: do the right thing, say the right thing and, good heavens, what would the neighbours think?

That's a lot of pressure on youngsters. Our parents projected their expectations on to us, and probably thereby created the worrier that I am today.

People always say that worrying and regret constitute two of the most useless wastes of time. You can't predict the future, so why worry about it? And you certainly can't fix the past, so *fugeddaboutit*. But think about it. Have you ever said something or not said something, and regretted it either way? It's true you never have to take back what you haven't said to begin with, but who thinks of that in the crucial moment?

And I for one can *what if* myself to death. I need to remember what my mom would always say, "You'll cross that bridge when you come to it." What if I get the job? How will I work all those hours in the hotel business? What if I don't get the job at all? Then what? My mom would say, "If this job came along, another one will come along too. Don't worry, there will be others." Which crystal ball was she looking into, I'd like to know.

When things got really out of hand and I was already celebrating something that had not happened, like a job offer, or meeting the man of my dreams, my mom would bring me back down to earth with, *get out of the buggy, Becky; you're not there yet*. This was the tail end of a story from her own youth. When friends of hers in their teens would daydream about being married and having little ones, some wise adult would pronounce those words to them, which just meant, *don't count the proverbial chickens before they hatch*.

It's hard not to wonder what the future holds. It's harder to recognize the mistakes you made in the past. Wise psychologists would say you did the best you could with what you knew at the time. While my mom didn't worry about the future, she sure spent plenty of time regretting past mistakes. So much so that I would refer to her behind her back as one of the Regret Sisters (see chapter 32).

There is a special art to worrying—regret's cousin. You can do it any time at all, on the subway, while falling asleep, as you wash the kitchen floor, or while doing the dishes. In fact, you can do it all of a sudden and say something out of the blue to your unsuspecting spouse right in the middle of a conversation. We can be having a chat about one thing and, all of a sudden, I will veer off into one of my worries as if we had been discussing it all along. "For heaven's sakes," my husband will say, "could you please put on your turn signal when you're changing directions?" Talk about tangent 101! Without any notice at all, I can suddenly go back to obsessing about something that has been recently bothering me. Worrying can fill up a lot of time. I wonder what would happen if I confined my worrying to just a few specific minutes a day, and spent the rest of my time actually living in the present instead of in the future. I think I will try that . . . but then I worry that I may not have allotted enough time to fully explore my worries.

41

Christmas... a time of giving, even if it's not our holiday

My parents were both very committed to community and, as a result, I had a strong sense of community too — to not only belonging and fitting in but also helping others. At Christmas time, which I loved even though it was not our holiday, there was always a flurry of activity in our household as my mom scrambled to find the perfect gift for each person on her list. Usually, although not always, Chanukah came earlier, so at least her hunt for gifts for us kids was over and done with. And, unlike in my own adult family years later, they didn't have a daughter born right before Christmas, thus making the mad scramble for Chanukah gifts, and Christmas gifts for friends — yes, I inherited the giving gene — even crazier, with having to also hunt down the right birthday gift for my daughter.

While my dad was heading up the UNICEF city-wide Christmas-card program, my mom had compiled a long list of those who they wished to repay for kindnesses shown during the year, especially among the medical community who, in the years before OHIP (Ontario Health Insurance Plan), never charged each other for services rendered. That went for kids, too. Had we owned a dog back then, I wonder if the same gift giving would extend to the veterinarian as well. It was small-town living at its most caring, and there was a whirlwind of parties to attend and to host, involving a huge amount of cooking and baking. And did I mention this is not *our* holiday?

With all the lights on the outside and inside of the homes along our street, and the laughter in our own living room, and hundreds of cards fighting for space on our mantel, it was hard not to get caught up in the spirit of it all. On Christmas Eve I was sure I heard Santa flying overhead. Even Christmas Day had a nice holiday vibe to it, not least of which was because there followed two weeks with no school. Our neighbours delivered chocolate Santas to us kids, and to this day I still deliver chocolate Santas to our neighbours' kids.

It is hard not to follow the example my parents set. Every year I put together a combined Chanukah, Christmas and birthday hit list. I acknowledge all the professionals who have provided us with excellent service all year long, including the veterinarian (nothing chocolate though in case the dogs get into it), the family doc and always something for her staff who answer the phone and make the appointments. What better way to ensure you get to the top of the list when you have developed a really bad sore throat or a mysterious rash? The dentist requires extra effort, as giving sweets would be a bit like laughing in his face. Then there is the physiotherapist, the city workers who pick up the trash, the snow-removal guy and the mailman (yes, ours is actually male). My parcels are always hand delivered or left carefully on my front porch. Who knew anyone could be so grateful for heavy socks? I have to admit, when I asked him what he wanted for Christmas, in a heavy accent he answered, "Sex." I was sure I must have heard this wrong, "Well, I'm not putting that in our mailbox," I replied, to give him an out and to buy me some time. Sure enough, he quickly corrected himself. "Socks, I meant socks." I have to admit it was funny, though.

The gift list goes on, but the point is that I think we learn a lot from what our parents say, and even more from watching what they do. Their generosity is what I grew up with, and the old saying, *children learn what they live*, became their lasting legacy.

As a grown-up, so as not to feel left out and to get into the holiday spirit, my tradition has always been to go out for dinner on Christmas Eve. When my daughter was young, we used to head out for a Christmas Eve drive — with my mom, of course — to view all the pretty displays of lights, and then on to dinner at a favourite place, one of a very few open on that particular night. On Christmas Day we would prepare a turkey breast with stuffing and a platter loaded with all kinds of festive goodies. My mom would bring along fruit cake too. So who says you have to be Christian to have fun on this particular holiday?

I'm grateful to my parents for so much, as they are so much of who I am today. I confess though, when the big day actually arrives, after that traditional Christmas Eve dinner, which my husband and I still do, we hole up in our house and watch movies. We don't see another soul for Christmas Day or Boxing Day. And that is a new tradition all our own. Time devoted to each other and to no one else. We've now added roast duck to our Christmas Day menu, as it is one of my husband's favourite dishes. Yes, we have our own little traditions that provide comfort and something to look forward to and, therefore, I never resent the fact that Christmas is not our holiday. Giving and just getting into the spirit are my own way of feeling included.

42

Cabbage rolls hold many secrets

Can this *giving* thing go too far? This is a question I find myself asking as I recall the past month or so. Yes, it is Christmas, Chanukah, and also family birthday time. Yes, our granddaughter was born five weeks ago, at one pound, fourteen ounces, which sent everyone else into a tailspin and me into the kitchen. But after four weeks of standing on my feet, cooking for the new parents, I suddenly realized my back was giving out.

If I didn't have the good sense to know when enough was enough, my back was certainly ready to quit, and it let me know in no uncertain terms. I couldn't find a comfortable place for myself. Sitting was no good. Standing was worse. Walking helped but, after about twelve thousand steps and a very happy doggie, how much more can you take? Sleep was an impossibility, either from not being able to turn over to get comfortable or from my mind wandering into the land of *what if* . . . neither of which was positive. Something we learn as we get older is that parents are only as happy as their most unhappy offspring. Corollary to that is when their child is worried, even a forty-year-old child, they worry too. And then, of course, there was my mother's admonishment when she was ninety and I was in my fifties, "Put on a sweater. I'm cold." It never ends.

Knowing that my back would not get better on muscle relaxants and pain meds, I sought out my trusty physiotherapist, whom my mother had consulted with for about twenty-five years. I, too, have gone to her for about twenty-something years, and over those years she has regaled me with many stories about my mom that I would never otherwise have known. Quite an eye-opener they were too.

There I am, working on back exercises, and receiving ultrasound therapy and a few other unpronounceable treatments, when the subject of Christmas comes up. "You don't by chance know how to make cabbage rolls, do you?" she suddenly asked. I replied, "I've never made them myself, but I have my grandmother's recipe." Without her specifically asking, I knew this was the one thing my physiotherapist now wanted for Christmas. No sooner do I leave her office than I am off to the grocery store, seeking out a cabbage, tomatoes, beef and all the other ingredients listed in my grandmother's recipe book. Her cabbage rolls were legendary but I had never made any. Never mind, I would give it a try.

I had heard that you can make life easier if you store the cabbage in the freezer, as its leaves will come off much more easily then. But no one bothered to mention to me that you need to thaw the cabbage for a day for this method to work. Unfortunately, I did not have a day available. My hope was that my physiotherapist would have a cancellation and I could then get in to see her before Christmas, which meant sometime the following day. There I was in my kitchen, putting a hot dish towel over my beloved cabbage's head in the hopes that I could, layer by layer, get the cabbage leaves peeled. Instead, I looked more like a hairdresser patting a client dry.

The process took me all day, but by five p.m. I had eighteen cabbage leaves ready to go. It was then I noticed that the recipe included no specific quantities of brown sugar, raisins, beets, prunes, etc., to go into the sauce — requiring a review of any and all cookbooks on my shelf that made some mention of cabbage rolls.

My mom cooked by instinct, a talent she applied to life in general. Me, I need specifics. How many breadcrumbs? How much sour salt? But none of this was indicated, so I took the best of all the recipes I could find and simply put the concoctions together. After all the stuffing and rolling and baking, I must admit the cabbage rolls smelled pretty good.

Mom always sampled everything she concocted before serving it to a guest. Even a masterful cake would have a tiny slice removed. We could pretend that it was a clever way of accommodating a cake knife, but those of us in mom's inner sanctum knew better. She just wanted to make sure it was perfect. So, a chip off the old block, I decided to try one little taste. Instantly memories of my mother, her wonderful cooking, and the aromas of our kitchen came flooding back. *One* brief taste. I'm glad I didn't eat the whole thing, as I would have had a memory meltdown.

I was telling this story to a good friend later that evening, and she began howling with laughter. She said, "Only you would be going to physio because of a sore back from all the cooking you did for the kids, then turn around and make cabbage rolls for the physiotherapist — so you have to go right back to her for treatment." What's wrong with this picture? What's wrong with me that I should think it my personal responsibility to prepare cabbage rolls so that my physiotherapist's Christmas dinner would be complete?

The office never did call me with a cancellation so they could squeeze me in today. Oh well, on Christmas Eve I will still be ready, with cabbage rolls in hand.

43

Twenty-twenty hindsight

Is it any wonder the confidence we gain as a child and the confidence we possess as we grow up are not one and the same? We come into the world with the best of intentions and we are pretty okay with ourselves. Then along comes life, and it has other ideas.

For some reason I was thinking back to my early childhood days in nursery school, where I remember standing before an easel, slathering paint onto paper, and when asked what the image was, replying, "A beast." Therapists no doubt would have a field day with that one. I also remember our little gray mats for nap time and, when we woke up, juice in little plastic cups. They were green, red, yellow or orange, and filled with the juice of the day: apple, orange, tomato, pineapple or grapefruit. I even remember the swings outside in the little playground, which were a bit too big for me.

On my first day at kindergarten I was afraid to leave my mother's side; no big surprise there. I had a little locker for my few little possessions, and it had a smiling yellow duck on the door.

We sat in groups gathered around tables and there was water play with boats, colouring with buckets full of crayons, and all manner of other exciting things for our little minds and hands to explore. I was busy colouring with a green crayon — who remembers this kind of minutiae? I do, obviously — and, all of a sudden, the green crayon broke in half. I was about to burst into tears when some other child pronounced with great authority, "Now you're gonna get it." I was terrified at that point, and I feel my heart speeding up as I write this. I think I've probably spent the rest of my life waiting for the other shoe to drop, so to speak.

No one said a word about the broken crayon, but from that moment on I felt that at any moment the proverbial tap on the shoulder was about to come. "Step into my office, please. What did you do? How could you?"

With hindsight today, after my university education in sociology, psychology and education, I know that such a remark can be delivered by a child from an abusive home, who is "gonna get it" no matter what the infraction. Thankfully, I myself did not come from such a home, and looking back with adult eyes, I feel sorry for that kindergartener. However, the remark hit home to the point that I lived my whole life in fear that someone would discover my misdeed, that I was a fraud, I was never good enough, never going to get that job, or receive that A on an assignment, or secure that date, or that . . . you name it. I was not good enough.

It's a miracle that, with all the natural knocks in our lives, any of us end up whole, sane or with any self-confidence at all. I marvel at my daughter's ability to stand up before audiences of any size and perform, appearing confident, brave and with more courage than I could ever muster. Where did she learn this?

There's an old adage that says, "You can't have confident, secure children when their parents have little self-esteem." Maybe I make too much of this, but I cringe when I hear other parents say to their little ones, "You're too slow. You're too clumsy.

You'll fall in so don't get too close to the water. You are such a klutz!" The list goes on.

I don't remember hearing those words myself as a child. No, it was more subtle. "Oh, how could you? How could you get such an awful mark in your arithmetic test?" — as if my parents' own reputation in the community was at stake because I had only got 64 per cent on a math test.

Parenting has changed over time, but I am still sensitive regarding what is being said and by whom when it involves little ones. I myself always try to find something positive to say. "He's not slow. He's motoring as fast as his tiny little legs can manage. Remember, he's not even two yet." Instead tell him something that makes him proud about walking at all. "Look how big you are. Last year you were just a little baby and you couldn't even walk. In fact, you were just learning to turn over in your crib." Okay, maybe that would be overkill.

Everyone has twenty-twenty hindsight. Much as I promised myself I would never make the same mistakes as my parents did, that I would actually listen to my children, that I would be attentive, that I would spend proper time with them, I wouldn't scold them for being loud or just having fun, nevertheless I would make other mistakes. And there are plenty of those to go around.

Why is it that we parents have such difficulty in listening and really hearing what our children are asking us? Are we too busy with our own agendas? Do we need our kids to become little replicas of us parents? It takes a really terrific parent to let their child simply *be*. Remember Dr. Spock? "Love them and leave them alone." Did any of us parents ever actually do that? Or were we all a bunch of control freaks hovering over our kids' every move?

No one wants to look back and admit, "Oh, we were really bad at parenting." Everyone has very good intentions. The truly confident kids are either very lucky or they fought very hard against the odds. I remember going shoe shopping once with my mother. All I wanted was a pair of desert boots, as everyone else was wearing them. So why did I have to have something different? And why did my mom then guilt me into buying what she herself thought would look nice on my feet? They were my feet after all.

Learning how and when to stand up to one's parents is an art all on its own and I just wasn't good at it. I settled for what my mom wanted instead of what I knew I wanted myself. Then I began to doubt my own decisions. I really wanted a green swamp coat, like every other girl in my class. All I really wanted was to fit in. But, no, I had to have something more in line with what my mom would have wanted when she herself was a child. And I really didn't want that. My first pair of blue jeans at age sixteen were indeed blue, but they weren't denim jeans. They were just a powder-blue pair of pants. Imposters. Oh, the shame of having a pair of blue pants and not the desired blue jeans. Does anyone wear anything else than the latter today? How hard would it have been just to listen to what *I* wanted?

It's these battles that are tiny in the adult's eyes but huge in a child's. Wouldn't it be better to be confident in your own choices, knowing that someone was listening to you and respecting your wishes?

To my mind, there is no more difficult job in the world than being a parent. In completing the circle, you only need to know how hard it was for your parents when you eventually become one yourself, and therein is the beginning of forgiveness. I know how much I valued my mother's wisdom and advice, and I deeply wish she were still here today. For the longest time after she passed away, I couldn't go out shopping, for she had become my shopping buddy over the years. Not in the early days when I was constantly trying to define myself and separate from her, but in later years, when we had begun to have fun together, it was her discerning eye and advice I always sought.

Not long ago, when shopping was still something we could do unmasked and unencumbered by a sense of guilt at needing anything from a store at all, I was inspecting a little black dress in a department store. I wasn't sure how it looked on me, but there was an older woman sitting in the dressing-room area with her own grown-up daughter. I said to the daughter, "My mom always went shopping with me and now I miss her advice. Your mom reminds me of my own. Mind if I borrow her opinion for a minute?" She seemed delighted. Her mom then said the dress was perfect for me and that, no, it did not make me look fat and was really quite flattering. I was so appreciative of her mom-like advice.

It's bizarre how when we are young, our parents have all these opinions that we don't want. And then, by the time we appreciate how valuable they really are, they are gone. If only we had known then what we know now, how we would cherish those moments, and maybe wouldn't have protested so much.

44

Once again it is Passover

Where has this year gone? As all of us who are making our way through a pandemic know, it has not been easy. For those who have lost loved ones and have felt helpless to do anything about it, it has been truly awful. "Not easy to make the best of it," as my mom would say. There is never any *best* in the face of something so unexpected and life-changing. Life can be devastating, and downright cruel at worst. And, still, life goes on. The seasons change. And here I am, creating another virtual Passover seder to be conducted on Zoom. Wish I could also figure out how to get Zoom to cook for me.

    I have spent the past two weeks in the kitchen, which I admit is one of my favourite places to be, just not under duress. There is a deadline to meet and dishes to switch, not to mention pots and pans, kosher-for-Passover food to buy and cupboards to clean and change over, all for only eight days. Maybe it's just a synonym for spring cleaning but, as we retell the Passover story — the exodus from Egypt — at the seder, it is clearly much more than that. It's as much about tenacity and perseverance as it is about holding true to our traditions.

Today many have altered how they mark this holiday, and so the details of observance vary from one house to another depending on your family's traditions. It's now either celebrating or commiserating, as the case may be.

Despite all the modern conveniences, it is a lot of work. I think of my mom grinding the meat by hand to make her famous chopped liver — or rather her mother's famous chopped liver. Don't even ask me for the ingredients, as you have to be willed the recipe from a previous generation. I am quite enamored of my food processor that, with the push of a button, rapidly does my bidding. Some recipes, like angel food cake, still take a lot of work with a handheld mixer; and if your kitchen is too hot, or the egg whites don't beat, forget about the parfait glasses. They aren't kosher for Passover. Did I mention the minimum eight to ten dozen eggs required for this holiday? And that's just for a family of two! It's not called the Festival of Cholesterol for nothing.

It is at this time of year that I miss my mom the most. Partly because when you marry into a large family seders cans include as many as forty people, which can sometimes feel overwhelming. By comparison, my family of origin was very small, but it was still familiar and it was mine just like those recipes.

My mom was always very considerate. She was concerned about phoning someone at the wrong time, even me, so she would keep the conversation to a minimum, sounding like she was permanently in a rush — or that I was — but now I realize she didn't want to intrude. I learned from my own daughter to take as much time as one needs, as there is no more important thing to do. I understand now that our mom was trying to be respectful of my time. And how I wish I could have reassured her then that I had all the time in the world for her, and how I wish I could pass that lesson on to my own children. Take the time now, as some day you won't have it. You will have some good memories, and maybe some excellent conversations with that parent whose impact may never leave you, but any real time together is precious and fleeting.

Passover lasts eight days and, true to form, even as our mother was failing, she was once again being considerate of my time. Not wanting to ruin this particular holiday for us forever, she waited until three days after Passover ended before she succumbed to congestive heart failure. Her heart may have failed, but mine was broken. It was too soon. I wasn't ready. I had more to share with her. I needed more time. I felt sure of that.

As mom herself would say, "That's how it goes, baby." Her best legacy to us was her passion for cooking. Her recipes, even though they were occasionally missing the precise details when relayed to us, were always delicious. Through trial and error, we then figured out the right amounts of this and that, and the right length of time to mix, stir, add, bake and doctor. My sister thus became a professional, natural chef. An over-achiever.

I myself absorbed mom's lessons about how to make the best of everything. I'm never afraid to serve company (when we can entertain again), however the dish turns out. So what if the brisket is in tiny shreds? How inspired is pulled brisket for Passover? Okay, you have to eat it on *matzoh,* not on a bun, but the key was that if it didn't turn out right, we had watched our mom find a solution to make it even better. Add another layer to the cake, mix it all together and say it's a trifle, disguising it with berries. Isn't this what life teaches us? Pondering whether it requires icing, it is always better to try that rather than just tossing it in the garbage.

So, mom, I am heading back into the kitchen to make more of your recipes to share with the kids, so we can all eat together and enjoy the Passover seder on Zoom. I really wish you were here to share it with us.

Thanks for the recipes. I will treasure them forever. By the way, your recipe never said when to put the cherry jam into the matzo farfel pudding. Do you mix it in with all the ingredients or do you dab some on just before it goes into the oven?

45

The truth about memory

Everyone has memories of their childhood: some good, some not so good and some so traumatic that they are blocked out completely. The thing about childhood memory that we must ask ourselves is, just how good was it? Can my memory really be trusted?

When I was visiting my aunt in Israel many years ago, I asked her about something from her own childhood. Why did she never deliver her brother — my uncle — his lunch when he was working out in the fields in what was then called the Old Country?

She responded by telling me about how big the crows were. What? My uncle had complained bitterly, even in his eighties, how his little sister, whose chore it was to bring him lunch every day, never brought him his food. He was hard at work in the fields and he felt hungry. Where was his lunch? Did she eat it herself? Sell it to someone else? What happened to it? As my aunt explained to me all those years later, the crows were as big or bigger than she was and she was so terrified of them that there was no way she was going to take Herschel his lunch. Sounds reasonable and it makes a good story.

I asked her another question and she answered, "Give me a minute. My shelves are very full but I will find it." She, of course, was referring to the shelves in her brain. If the older we get, the more we have on our shelves, no wonder we have a hard time finding the precise memory we are seeking. Does it stand to reason that, as youngsters with nothing on our shelves, our memories are crystal clear? I don't think so. But then why is it that I can name every student in my Grade two class, but, if I meet you today at the grocery store, I might not remember I met you just yesterday on the street? And if you change your clothes or your hairstyle, I am seemingly doomed to forget who you are.

This memory business has gotten me thinking. Why do I remember a childhood mostly filled with fun? Am I deliberately choosing to remember it that way? My sister, however, remembers a childhood filled with pressure. I guess I was lucky then to be the second-born. All the practice runs were carried out on her, so when I came along, either no one cared as much or it was easy by that time. Practice makes perfect, right? So, you would think the second-born would be perfect. Not so. I think far less was expected of me than of my sister. Or maybe when my mom fell down the back stairs late in her first pregnancy, my sister got damaged on the way down. I can joke about this now since clearly neither my mom nor my sister got hurt in the fall, just frightened.

Our childhood reminiscences are completely different. The idea for this book came about as a result of the many times during a conversation when my sister would say, "I have no recollection of that." Or she would ask, "Why were we there? "What do you remember about . . . ?" I try to fill in the blanks for her with my memories, but personal perception probably has a huge impact on what we each remember and why we remember it. And now my shelves are getting "quite full," as my aunt would say, and that's no longer so easy. My childhood is still crystal-clear in my mind, but my immediate past not so much.

Children experience their growing-up years in different ways. Much has been written about the importance of birth order, the age of parents at the time of birth and their financial circumstances. I suspect if you were to interview four children from the same family about their childhood years, they would all have different stories to tell. I myself wanted to tell a few of them before I got too old and grey.

Keeping in mind that perception is everything, and that every story has more than one side to it, this book is written for my sister, whom I love dearly. Of course, it is written from my perspective, and these are my own memories. I just hope it helps jog some of the better ones for her.

P.S. Mom and dad really did love me more!

Afterword

My sister and I used to joke about writing a cookbook called "It All Ends Up in a Parfait Glass." Sorry, Sis. Even though you are the one with the natural chef designation, this title was too perfect for mom's recipes for life, not just the ones for her kitchen.

Sitting down to write about my childhood memories made me take stock of a time when our parents were the ultimate authority on how to be in the world. As I grew up and learned that the world was so much larger than our very small existence, I realized how fortunate we kids were.

In writing these stories and re-engaging with my youth, I discovered how complex an individual our mom was. Not only were there multiple ways to interpret her words, she also reserved the right to choose which parts of her own advice she followed. The axiom "Do as I say, not as I do" comes to mind.

The other lesson I learned from looking back at childhood is that parents aren't perfect. While we vow never to make the same mistakes with our own children, it's not long before we are busy making new ones. I figure if I wish to be forgiven for my mistakes, I must forgive my parents theirs. After all, neither children nor life come with instructions. Just like a parfait, the end result is a bit of a mishmash. Fortunately, we didn't turn out too badly.

We learned some lifelong lessons the hard way, such as the old "Good judgment comes from experience, and experience comes from bad judgment." Other lessons were learned by coincidence and happenstance, and still others by example. While my mother's sayings inspired us and amused us, it is the wisdom within that I am still pondering today. And they thought we weren't listening!

Here's where I'll bring in another old adage, whose wisdom has never been truer: "The older I got, the smarter my parents became." As I get older, it is my mother's wisdom I miss by ever-increasing degrees, and which I could only appreciate long after she was gone. Isn't that always the way?

END

Acknowledgements

Imagining these stories would ever come together in a book was both exhilarating and daunting. For making the process a little less intimidating, I was fortunate to have friends, family and colleagues cheering me on.

Barbara Snelgrove, my first reader, for providing eagle eyes, sensitivity to all issues current and support throughout.

Judy Cipin, my friend and steadfast lifelong sounding board, for her encouragement as the writing progressed.

Eleanor Minuk for helping me revise, reword and rethink my ideas and for her input on the big decisions in life and in the book.

The many friends and family members who were so generous with their wisdom and stories.

Author Tom Taylor for sharing his thoughts, experience and contacts in the publishing process.

Marial Shea, the most talented editor I have ever had the pleasure of working with — thank you for making my words sing, for adding polish and poise to the finished product.

Marilyn Herbert for her review and letting me know I could breathe out, that my scribblings would resonate.

Julie Cohn for her enthusiasm for the book and for letting me know these stories were truly funny, poignant and worth telling.

Joel Rosenberg, for your steadfast love and support, for keeping me grounded and for listening with your heart from the first word to the last.

Ellie Zacks, my sister, whose relentless questions about our past was the inspiration for these stories and made me want to get them all down on paper so she would have memories to keep, even if mine are a wee bit different from yours.

Lastly, to my parents, Adelyn and Louis Zacks, without whom there would be no stories to tell. Wherever you are, I hope you'll agree that maybe after all this time I might have actually accomplished something.

About the Author

MARJIE ZACKS grew up in Peterborough, Ontario, then moved to Ottawa, Ontario. She has a Bachelor of Arts from York University and a Master of Arts in education from Central Michigan University. After thirty-eight years in public relations in both corporate and not-for-profit sectors, she is happily retired. She lives in the Toronto area with her husband and their much adored and very well-behaved Soft-Coated Wheaten Terrier. She is also mom to four adult children and "Bubby" to three grandchildren. This is her first book.

My sister, Ellie, Mom, Dad, and me.

www.ingramcontent.com/pod-product-compliance
Lightning Source LLC
Chambersburg PA
CBHW060400080526
44583CB00012B/397